CREATING
You & Co.

**LEARN TO THINK
LIKE THE CEO OF YOUR
OWN CAREER**

WILLIAM BRIDGES

DA CAPO PRESS
A Member of the Perseus Books Group

Library of Congress Catalog Card Number: 98-87225

ISBN-10: 0-7382-0032-8   ISBN-13: 978-0-7382-0032-3

Da Capo Press is a member of the Perseus Books Group

Cover design by Suzanne Heiser
Text design by Diane Levy
Set in 11-point ITC New Baskerville by NK Graphics

First paperback printing, October 1998

Find us on the World Wide Web
www.dacapopress.com

Da Capo Press books are available at special discounts for bulk purchases in the U.S. by corporations, institutions, and other organizations. For more information, please contact the Special Markets Departments at the Perseus Books Group, 11 Cambridge Center, Cambridge MA 02142 or call (800) 255-1514 or (617) 252-5298 or email special.sales@perseusbooks.com

CREATING

You & Co.

OTHER BOOKS BY WILLIAM BRIDGES

JobShift: How to Prosper in a Workplace Without Jobs

Transitions: Making Sense of Life's Changes

Managing Transitions: Making the Most of Change

Surviving Corporate Transition: Rational Management in a World of Mergers, Layoffs, Start-Ups, Takeovers, Divestitures, Deregulation, and New Technologies

The Character of Organizations: Using Jungian Type in Organizational Development

A Year in the Life

Contents

Foreword:
A Message to the Reader

We must all obey the great law of change. It is the most powerful law of nature.

—EDMUND BURKE

This is not a book about finding a job. No, there are enough of those. This is a book on finding *work*—work that both satisfies and supports you. I didn't write this book for people without a job—although they too will find it useful—but for people who, whether or not they're traditionally employed, feel the lack of fulfilling work and a career taking them where they want to go. My hope is that if you are such a person, you can use *Creating You & Co.* to renew your career by rebuilding it on the only two bases that can endure: the market's needs and your own resources.

As you'll see in Chapter 1, looking for a *job* is the wrong way to go about finding work or renewing your career, because jobs are disappearing. That is because in our fast-moving, high-tech information age, they are no longer the best way of getting work done. Many of the kinds of successful organizations that you wish you could work for are already getting their work done without much reliance on jobs.

When you look for a *job,* you are looking for something that is fading from the socioeconomic picture because it is past its evolutionary prime.

I laid out the decline-of-the-job thesis in *JobShift*. My intent here is to provide you with practical help based on those ideas. This book is a do-it-yourself career development program.

To grasp the opportunities that are really present, you have to understand that jobs were products of the Industrial Revolution and the kinds of work that characterized that time. Before 1800 or so, no one had ever had a job. The word *job* didn't refer to something you could "have," but rather to something you "did." For centuries, "job" had meant a task or piece of work. There was no such thing as job security, because the traditional job was, by definition, here today and gone tomorrow. Right now your job might be to get in the hay before it rained. Tomorrow your job might be to make a pair of shoes for your young daughter, and the next day it could be to take the cheese your family had made and sell it at the fair in the nearby town. At the end of the week, your job could be to repair the roof on north side of your house. You "did" jobs.

But with the coming of industrialism, people migrated away from that world to the factory. Work was organized very differently there. Factory workers found themselves with a new kind of job, not just because it involved tending a machine but because in the factory, the manufacturing process was cut up into many separate segments or functions, each of which was given to a person to do over and over again in the same way every day. Jobs had job descriptions (at first implicitly and then explicitly), and your job was yours while the next one was somebody else's, like little pieces of property. People "had" jobs now. It was only a matter of time before people began to feel that, like property, they owned their jobs.

After almost two centuries of having jobs, the landscape of the workplace is again being transformed. For all the reasons we will discuss in the next chapter, the work of the Information Age does not lend itself to "jobs" as neatly as industrial work did. Companies that are still hiring people to do jobs, paying them on the basis of how they do them, supervising them to be sure that they are doing them, and organizing their workers in a hierarchy of jobs are finding that they are operating with a handicap. On the other hand, companies like Intel, CNN, and EDS have largely abandoned jobs and are thriving.

Jobs were one of the most important products of the Industrial Age, and they fit the characteristics of that world, namely:

- readily separated functions and areas of responsibility
- linear work processes that were easy to segment
- long sequences of predictable activity
- discrete and relatively infrequent changes

Jobs were created because they were the most effective ways of getting work done in the world that created them. They aren't so effective today because the way we are most productive has changed. That is why they are being replaced by temporary work, outsourced work, the use of consultants, cross-trained teams, or self-managed telecommuters.

That's why a job is largely a short-term solution to an individual's vocational problems and why looking for one these days is so frustrating. A better course of action is to find the work that actually needs doing and present yourself to whoever needs it as the best way to get it done. This is the way in which people have instinctively been finding the best opportunities for some time—those "how did she ever find that position?" cases that we all marvel at.

My purpose in this book is to lay out a practical path toward such ideal work situations. It is one that you can readily follow. Based on the reality of a workplace that is being systematically and rapidly "dejobbed" (the subject of Chapter 1), the book shows you how to take the four steps necessary to take advantage of the great postindustrial jobshift:

1. How to discover and describe the unique mix of resources that you bring to the new workplace (Chapters 2–6).

2. How to develop an eye for markets and use it to search this workplace for the best places to apply your resources (Chapter 7).

3. How to combine the personal data on your resources with the external information about opportunities into a viable "product" (Chapter 8).

4. How to reinvent your career as a one-person business, built around the creation and delivery of that product (Chapter 9), and how to formulate a practical plan to develop that business (Chapter 10).

The goal of this four-step process is not simply understanding and new attitudes but a to-do list of actions that you can begin to take as soon as you put down the book. You will not be able to remake your career quickly. Like a huge ship, it's going to take a while to turn around. But you can get started right away and see the first results very soon.

A generation from now, many of the things that we are talking about are going to seem pretty obvious. It may even be that young people will come out of school with full-blown plans to find places for themselves in a world without jobs. We'll talk in the Afterword about changes that are likely to take place in education, as well as those in labor unions, government services, corporations, and nonprofit organizations. It may be that some readers will find the work that best suits them in changing those very institutions. There is work there that is begging to be done, and those institutions could provide us with the kinds of training and assistance that we so much need.

For the time being, however, individuals will be largely on their own. That is the reason for this book. It is a map for your journey. It is a blueprint for turning you the individual into "You & Co." That doesn't mean forcing you to form alliances or incorporate yourself. Rather, I propose to show you how to identify and harness the resources you have, just as a CEO does for a company. The result may turn out to be a one-person operation, or a growing corporation, or simply a new relationship with your current employer. However you shape your future, the important lesson is that you will be shaping it yourself rather than trying to fit into a box defined by someone else.

I've drawn the lessons in *Creating You & Co.* from both research and my own experience. Back in 1974 I left my last regular job—as a professor of literature—and headed off to do something new. I had no idea where I would end up. Worse, I had no idea which way to head. I was caught in a logical trap that went (in my particular case) like this:

What do you want to do?

Quit teaching literature.

What are you trained to do?

Teach literature.

What do you have experience in doing?

Teaching literature.

In what field do you have a network of support?

The teaching of literature.

You probably have your own version of that maddening inner Q&A session.

I've learned a good deal about career renewal since then, and I'll be passing it on as I go. But the first thing I learned is that the confusion so many people feel when they think of what they want to do with their lives is that they confuse work with jobs. (If it's not a job, then it's *volunteer work*—right?) We're a job-minded people. We hardly know how else to think about work than to talk of our looking for jobs, the government creating jobs, corporations sending jobs overseas, labor unions protecting jobs, and our educational system preparing people for tomorrow's jobs.

A generation ago, the legal scholar Thurman Arnold said that people "believe that a society is disintegrating when it can no longer be pictured in familiar terms. Unhappy is a people that has run out of words to describe what is going on." It's time we found a new way to think and talk about work, for until we do, we'll see no hope for ourselves and our children. It's a completely doable task. The clues and signs are everywhere—in how people are actually finding wonderful work situations and in how innovative organizations are already getting work done. The bad news is that, like all large societal changes, it is requiring us to abandon the vehicles that got us this far and strike out on foot for a while. And that is a frightening prospect.

When you have to do that, a map helps. This book is a map, and I hope that it helps you.

SEEING THE JOBSHIFT AT WORK

At the end of each of these chapters you will find questions, an inventory of some sort, or suggestions for activities. Here I'm going to offer you a short exercise designed to measure the forces that are dejobbing some organization that you know well. It may be the organization you work for as an employee, or it may be the little one-person organization that you grandly call "The XXXX Group." It may be the educational institution where you study, or it may be the church that you attend. It may be the company your spouse works for, or it may be a company where you used to work. Any organization that you know well will do.

Respond to each of the following twenty-five statements by circling the appropriate number, using the following scale to indicate your score:

4: strong agreement

3: moderate agreement

2: yes and no . . . not a clear picture, one way or the other

1: moderate disagreement

0: strong disagreement

1. In our organization, job descriptions are important. People try to ensure that whatever is done will be done by the appropriate person or department.

   4   3   2   1   0

2. Most people are grouped by functions, and cross-functional teams are relatively unimportant in the larger picture of how work gets done.

   4   3   2   1   0

3. Authority is mostly position-based rather than being dictated by the needs of a particular situation.

   4   3   2   1   0

4. Although we sometimes talk about rewarding innovation and the ability to deliver, we seldom really compensate and promote people on that basis.

   4   3   2   1   0

5. The leaders/managers of the organization aren't very effective spokespeople for the organization's vision and values; some of them give only half-hearted support.

   4   3   2   1   0

6. Most managers in the organization lead by words, not example. Too many of them don't really "walk their talk."

   4   3   2   1   0

7. When something has to be done in the organization, you often hear people arguing, "That isn't my job!"

   4   3   2   1   0

8. And you sometimes hear, "I'm just doing my job" as an excuse for doing something that doesn't really need to be done or that doesn't make sense.

   4   3   2   1   0

9. Temps don't do important work in this organization; they are used (if at all) to fill in for temporarily absent permanent workers.

   4   3   2   1   0

10. The organization doesn't use outsourcing very much; it prefers to use its own employees to do whatever needs to be done.

    4   3   2   1   0

11. The organization hasn't yet begun to use communications technology to help people to work from home, from a client's location, from a satellite facility, or while traveling.

    4   3   2   1   0

12. People in this organization have traditional "jobs," and anyone whose role doesn't clearly fit that mold is not in a very secure situation.

    4   3   2   1   0

13. There is not much real "empowerment" in the organization, though there may be some rhetoric about decentralizing decision making or authority.

    4   3   2   1   0

14. Below the executive level, few employees really understand the organization's financial situation or how their particular activity might affect it.

    4   3   2   1   0

15. If you asked people in the organization who their "clients" or "customers" are, you'd probably get a spotty response; even those who talk up customer service often don't practice it.

    4   3   2   1   0

16. Seniority and job title count for more than actual contribution in determining status and security in the organization.

    4   3   2   1   0

17. In any given 100-person unit within the organization, there would probably be more than three levels of management.

    4   3   2   1   0

18. There isn't a very strong entrepreneurial streak among employees, nor does the organization's culture support people who want to set up new ventures.

    4   3   2   1   0

19. The organization lacks internal resources to help employees find new ways to use their talents when their current jobs no longer need to be done.

    4   3   2   1   0

20. The organization insulates customers, suppliers, and subcontractors from its planning processes, and it doesn't share significant information about the future with them.

    4   3   2   1   0

21. Things change constantly within the organization.

    4   3   2   1   0

22. The organization's business is currently being affected by new technology and the introduction of new products.

    4   3   2   1   0

23. There is intense competition within the industry or profession to which the organization belongs.

    4   3   2   1   0

24. The organization is currently (or is seriously considering) utilizing Business Process Reengineering to redesign how it gets its work done.

    4   3   2   1   0

25. In the past three years, the organization has "downsized" by at least 10 percent, through layoffs, early retirement, or attrition.

    4   3   2   1   0

Now total your score on these twenty-five items. Your score was_____

As you probably guessed, the higher your score, the more likely it is that the organization will need to move away from jobs. That is especially so if the scores were high on both the last five questions (which measure the need to move away from jobs) and the first twenty questions (which measure the resistance to doing so). That particular combination is highly unstable and puts the organization—and your job-based employment—in real danger. Just why the answers to these different questions add up to a measure of the organization's health and prospects will be clear when you read Chapter 1.

PART ONE

WHY YOU NEED YOU & CO.

When old words die out on the tongue, new melodies break forth from the heart; and where the old tracks are lost, new country is revealed with its wonders.

—Rabindranath Tagore

The interval between the decay of the old and the formation and the establishment of the new consitutes a period of transition which must always necessarily be one of uncertainty, confusion, error, and wild and fierce enthusiasm.

—John C. Calhoun

Before you can put together your new career plan, you are going to have to understand two things: first, what is really happening in the workplace and second, how to assess your own resources for dealing with it.

First, what's going on out there? Yesterday's workers didn't have to understand *why* companies were hiring—only *whether* they were hiring. People used to say that you had to check your brain at the door when you came to work. But in fact you could check your brain before you even started looking for work. Today, however, the worker who does not understand *what* the organization is looking for, *why* it is looking, and *how* the work might be done doesn't know enough to find the work that is out there. This does not mean that you need to be a labor expert to find work. (In fact, labor experts are likely to be *jobs* experts.) It just means that you need to have a commonsense, realistic view of what is going on. A good beginning is to understand three things.

The first is how and why the workplace is changing. It isn't enough to generalize about "more competition." You need to understand the workplace for the same reason that an entrepreneur needs to understand the market: so that you can not only deal with the changes taking place but actually turn them to your advantage and capitalize on the opportunities that they provide.

Second, you need to understand why traditional jobs no longer fit this world and why companies are abandoning them. You may feel that you'd be more comfortable working in an organization that is still based on jobs, but you need to understand that even these organizations are no longer "secure" places to work in the way they used to be, because they are unlikely to be able to compete effectively against dejobbed companies for much longer. That nice "solid" job that you find in them is therefore built on sand. The whole idea of "risk" has changed. Except as a short-term expedient, it is now "risky" to depend on a conventional job in a company that uses such jobs to get its work done.

The third thing you need to understand is what the alternatives to jobs are. There are many other ways to work that can benefit both you and the organization. More and more organizations are getting their work done by means of such roles, and if you are looking for work and interested in building a career that has some longevity to it, you ought to be considering making them part of your plans.

Those are matters we'll take up in Chapter 1. Chapter 2 is devoted to how a person can assess the resources that he or she brings to this new workplace. Yesterday's worker did not have to worry much about doing that. There were "qualifications" for jobs. They were listed on the job postings or in the want ads. You could sometimes fast-talk your way past one or two of them, but that didn't happen often.

The whole idea of "qualifications" has changed, however. The organizations that are moving away from jobs are also moving away from traditional hiring practices. They are looking for different things, and you will need to understand what these things are in order to present yourself to them successfully. These new qualifications are the subject of Chapter 2.

CHAPTER ONE

Why It's So Hard to Find a Really Good Job

Just because a company like Digital [Equipment Corporation] doesn't have a job for you doesn't mean that it doesn't have work for you.

—MARK DRESNER, EXECUTIVE VICE PRESIDENT, INFINITE TECHNOLOGY AND "DOWNSIZED" DEC EMPLOYEE

WHAT'S GOING ON OUT THERE?

The idea that the world is changing at an unprecedented rate is one of those clichés that has passed through so many hands that much of its value has been rubbed off. But it is true all the same. More important, some of its most important implications are not yet widely understood. One of them is the ways in which frequent and far-reaching change is affecting our work lives.

The conventional view is that constant change keeps the organizational world in a perpetual churn. Company fortunes rise and fall, and jobs are created and destroyed in the process. Individual workers, like sailors on a storm-tossed ship, keep getting washed overboard, where they swim for their lives until they clamber onto another ship—only to be swept overboard in the next storm. Jobs—those times when workers have a solid deck under their feet—keep getting briefer and briefer in duration.

5

That view isn't entirely wrong, for layoffs do keep occurring and career segments have indeed become very brief for many workers. But the changes that affect us are not just the quantitative ones that can be traced in rising and falling employment figures or press accounts of downsizing. They are also—and more fundamentally—qualitative changes as well. Defining today's situation as a period of economic turbulence like those we have experienced periodically in the past fundamentally misinterprets the phenomenon that is transforming people's work lives beyond anything they could have imagined a decade ago.

THE HANDWRITING ON THE WALL

Consider the following situations, which might seem to have little in common except that they are all work-related and are taking place in many different places simultaneously.

- Chief economists at big banks and brokerage houses used to be sitting pretty: six-figure salaries and a critical skill that seemed to make their jobs safe. But then some economists who had lost or left their jobs got together and set up firms that provided sophisticated forecasts based on a consensus of many predictions—and did so for $500–$1,000 a year. *The plot line: A small-business product replaces a big-company employee and does it at less than 1 percent of the cost.*
- Carter's Gold Medal Soft Drinks, an English division of the Swiss food giant, Hero, needed to change its distribution and delivery system. Instead of hiring a consulting firm or looking for a new executive, the company went to Executives on Assignment, a temporary agency, and found Jon Tipping. He came in as a consultant might have and analyzed the situation, making recommendations for radical changes. And then he took over the role of distribution manager (as a temp would have) and put his own plan into operation. After saving the company 15 percent of it annual distribution costs, he hired his own replacement and left. *Plot line: A contract hire solves a company problem, implements the solution, and moves on.*
- When the World Trade Center was severely damaged by a terrorist bomb in February 1993, the company chosen to clean up the disaster site was Restoration Co. of Norcross, Georgia. In only a few days, the company increased its payroll from 50 to 3,600, set up a warehouse of

cleaning equipment, and created from scratch a sophisticated radio communications system. It did all of these things *and* completed the cleanup in a mere sixteen days—in spite of losing two days to an immense blizzard that brought New York City to a standstill! ***Plot line:*** *A very small company expands enough to do a huge job and then returns to its former size, all in less than three weeks.*

- Lotus, now part of IBM, has a manufacturing facility in North Reading, Massachusetts, which has only six full-time employees. They are a work team that produces software during slow times and a management team with 250 workers under them during busier times. Where do the 250 come from? Olsten Corp., a staffing firm, employs and trains them—supplying them to Lotus as needed: ***Plot line:*** *A few full-time workers can operate a facility if they have a full-scale staff on call, paying them only when there is work for them to do.*

- Boston-based Trinity Communications has forty employees, over half of whom used to work for Trinity's largest customer, the New England, a large life insurance company. In a major reorganization, that company closed down its Communications Department and then helped its core employees to start up as a freestanding business to which the New England contracted out most of its communications work. Other companies take a similarly encouraging attitude toward employees leaving, setting up businesses, and then taking on work from their former employer. Boeing Co. even runs a training program to prepare employees to do that. ***Plot line:*** *A company finds that its own workers can be more valuable as vendors than as regular employees.*

- When Johns Hopkins University decided to index its Medical Institutions Archives, it turned not to its own staff but to a company with the unlikely name of Electronic Scriptorium. Well, the name isn't so unlikely, really, since its employees were all monks at the Holy Cross Abbey in Virginia and the Gethsemani Abbey in Kentucky. Their vows kept them from working in the world, but not from doing the world's work in their cloistered institutions. ***Plot line:*** *The answer to the organization's problem may lie in outsourcing the work that it needs done to a company that capitalizes on its special resources.*

- And finally: when a subsidiary of Reuters Holdings, London, that designs computer screens needed people for a project, it "borrowed" them from a dozen other companies. These workers on loan were spread out geographically, so most of their work had to be done by e-mail and fax. In spite of that, they worked as a team to accomplish the work that Reuters needed done. ***Plot line:*** *Your workers today don't need to be on site or even employed by you. You just go after the best people to do the work and create the conditions under which they will get it done.*

What is the underlying theme that unites all of these stories? It is that more and more of the work that must be done today is being done by people who do not hold "jobs" at the company that needs the work done.

- They work for some other company to which the work is outsourced.
- They work in a role too ephemeral or too fluid to be called a regular job.
- They are self-employed and arrive on the doorstep as consultants or independent professionals.
- They are hired on a temporary or fixed-term basis.

With so much work diverted into these channels, it's no wonder that those solid, full-time, long-term jobs with yesterday's "good employers" are so hard to find.

But these examples are the results of causes that run much deeper and have changed the workplace for good, just as industrialism did almost two hundred years ago. The "dejobbing" of the modern organization is not taking place because of some movement or fad. It is the simple result of social and economic forces that are sweeping across the modern world like a climatic shift. These forces comprise six distinct aspects.

HOW AND WHY THE WORKPLACE IS CHANGING

The first of the forces that have changed the workplace stems from the fact that more and more of today's work involves the processing of knowledge rather than the manipulation of things. Even in companies that were at the heart of the industrial economy—auto manufacturing, for example—the majority of the workers do "knowledge work" rather than traditional industrial work. Marketing, research and development, finance, personnel, administration, information services, procurement, distribution—all these fields are dominated by knowledge work, even when the organization's product is industrial.

Peter Drucker has put the matter with his usual clarity and bluntness. Today, he argues,

> *the real, controlling resource and the absolutely decisive "factor of production" is now neither capital nor land nor labor. It is knowledge. Instead of capitalists and proletarians, the classes of the post-capitalist society are knowledge workers and service workers.*

What he does not note is that while we can talk about knowledge jobs and service jobs, the work involved in such jobs is far more difficult to parcel out into distinct job descriptions than traditional factory and office work was. Further, knowledge and service work are much more likely than industrial work to be done by cross-functional teams (where people have "assignments" rather than jobs) than is the physical work on an assembly line. Knowledge or service work is more likely to be turned over to consultants or independent professionals than is industrial work, and it is also easier to outsource. The bottom line: knowledge and, to a slightly lesser extent, service work blur the job boundaries that were so clear in the traditional factory and office.

The second factor causing dejobbing in today's workplace is information and communications technology. Knowledge work wouldn't be possible without computers, modems, fax machines, pagers, and cellular phones. It wouldn't be possible without the software that converts everything into digital data that can be stored, sorted, retrieved, and formatted in a way that pre-electronic information never could be.

Industrial technology concentrated people in time (regular hours and fixed shifts) and space (factories and offices). The lathes and looms and canners and conveyor belts allowed everyone to come together to get work done that they could not accomplish at home or in scattered shops. The new information technology, on the other hand, disperses them by enabling them to do their work anywhere and anytime. If you want a *job*, you probably need to be ready for eight to five or the swing shift and for a little cubicle on the third floor or a station on the assembly line. But if you want to *work*, it's what you produce that counts, not when and where you work.

Technology has also increased the pace of innovation, and that in turn means that no given work arrangement can last as long as it used to. New products follow one another so closely that organizations have to be reorganized constantly to be ready to produce the next generation of products. As cycle times get shorter, roles or organizational groupings that cannot be changed quickly and easily become handicaps.

The new technology also amplifies change. Communications technology increases our contact with novel situations by destroying the time and space buffers that used to limit our exposure to changes that took place elsewhere. Events that happened at a distance never used to enter people's awareness, because by the time people heard of them—if they ever did—they were old news. Today, the impact of events that happen on the other side of the world is felt almost as quickly here as there.

That fact brings us to the third major contributor to the movement away from jobs, the pace of change itself. Changes happen more frequently, and we experience more of them directly. The result is that, as Xerox CEO Paul Allaire has said,

Operating effectively in this more complex and volatile business environment requires the capacity to cope with change—and at a very rapid pace. . . . [We] have to create a new organizational architecture flexible enough to adapt to change. We want an organization that can evolve, that can modify itself as technology, skills, competitors, and the entire business change.

As we shall see in a moment, the job has proved to be a poor building block for this new architecture.

The search for this "new organizational architecture" brings us to the fourth force contributing to the dejobbing of our organizations, and that is the current spate of management-initiated efforts to build more flexibility, rapid response, customer focus, and individual accountability into the organization. Whether in the form of total quality management (TQM), customer service, empowerment, self-management, reengineering, or cross-training, management initiatives have shifted the focus from "doing your job" to "doing whatever needs to be done." What needs to be done includes anything that will

- ensure world-class quality (TQM)
- delight the customer (customer service)

- solve the problem (empowerment)
- decide what needs to be done (self-management)
- create effective and efficient business processes (reengineering)
- accomplish each other's tasks (cross-training)

Each of these initiatives is launched to accomplish something that everyone recognizes as important, but all of them end up eroding further the already unclear outlines of the traditional job.

A fifth contributor to dejobbing is the desire to create Allaire's "architecture flexible enough to adapt to change," which also leads to efforts to "de-integrate" or "unbundle" the organization into separable elements. You can see this impulse in the breakup of AT&T, Hilton Hotels Corporation, ITT, and other corporate entities. You can see the same impulse in the tendency to "disaggregate" formerly bundled functions or activities and reinvent them as separate profit centers. And you can see it in the movement to "deconstruct" the organization into separate operations, at least some of which can be outsourced to external providers or turned over to independent professionals who come into the company to do on contract what was formerly done by employees. In each case, the organization is disassembled into its component parts, and it thus becomes easier to find ways of accomplishing business and getting work done without depending on regular, full-time, long-term employees.

Sixth and finally, there's the force of the baby boom (there's always the baby boom!). It's the biggest demographic group in our history, an 800-pound gorilla in the menagerie of influences. Whatever the boomers are concerned about or interested in becomes, almost automatically, a major factor in any social or economic equation. Cheryl Russell, the former editor in chief of *American Demographics,* has said that the baby boomers' dominant characteristic is individualism (which she defines as an emphasis of self over group) and has called that "the master trend of our time."

Although she is apparently unaware of the socioeconomic shift that we are calling dejobbing, she calls the boomers "the first generation of free agents." The free-agent mentality leads to frustration with traditional jobs. A boomer's parents are always troubled by his or her readiness to leave a good job at a "solid" company for an ill-defined role in some little firm. Or, when they stay at the solid company, boomers work away at the boundaries of the job, pushing them out to bring in more challenge and freedom. In either case, the traditional job gives way to something looser, more flexible, and more transient.

Not only are the boomers' career aspirations contributing to the movement away from fixed and standardized jobs and toward more individualized ways of earning a living. The kinds of products and services that this generation favors also contribute to the job-eroding forces we have already identified. According to Russell, the boomers are "personalizing" the market and the whole economy in three different ways. They desire products and services that are (1) "custom-designed for and marketed to ever-smaller segments of consumers, even to the individual level"; (2) immediate ("successful businesses deliver products and services at the convenience of the consumer rather than the producer"); and (3) seen as having value ("businesses must price competitively or create innovative products that can command premium prices").

Now let's translate these market forces into the framework we are using. First, the production of a customized product or service makes it hard for workers to limit their efforts to the kinds of standardized activity that traditional job descriptions presume. Jobs grew out of mass production, and customized production represents a shift away from the traditional industrial roles. Second, the demand for immediacy and on-demand delivery simply intensifies that process. If it has to be done immediately, it will be harder for workers to say that they won't do it because it isn't their job. And finally, the demand for value means that every undertaking is in competition with dozens of others to deliver the value for which the individual customer will pay. As it gets more and more difficult for traditional products to hold on to their markets, it becomes correspondingly likelier that the traditional job will be replaced by something more flexible.

As the market full of boomers drives product innovations that require organizational changes, so the difficulty of maintaining market dominance leads to a constantly expanding number of suppliers. That proliferation of sources for goods and services further accelerates the changes we have been talking about. *Inc.* magazine writer John Case uses the metaphor of "friction" to describe the way in which the changes "free up" the market and destroy the old barriers to competition.

Economic friction is everything that keeps markets from working according to the textbook model of perfect competition: Distance. Cost. Restrictive regulations. Imperfect information. In high-friction markets, customers don't have many suppliers to choose among. . . . Low-friction markets are just the reverse. New competitors crop up all over, and customers are quick to respond. . . . The single most significant change in the economy over the past 20 years has been a wholesale reduction in friction.

And that same reduction in friction further speeds up change. It's a feedback loop that intensifies the effects that it creates, like the audio system that picks up its own sound and escalates it into an ear-splitting shriek.

WHY JOBS DON'T WORK ANYMORE

When people talk about how temps and part-timers are being used instead of traditional workers or how "good jobs" disappear when work is outsourced to external suppliers, they are usually suggesting that companies are simply and greedily trying to get away with not paying good wages. Now greed is real enough in the corporate world and always has been, but a better example of it can be found in the excessive money paid to top executives than in the movement away from jobs filled by full-time, long-term workers.

The fundamental reason that organizations are moving away from such jobs and such workers is their need to deal with the conditions just outlined above. Organizations today are desperately searching for that "architecture flexible enough to adapt to change" that Xerox's Allaire called for. And traditional jobs, quite simply, don't provide that flexibility and adaptiveness. An environment where change is the norm poses a number of problems in this respect.

1. Jobs and the job-oriented mindset encourage people to "do their jobs," but not to do "whatever needs doing." If what needs doing falls outside the narrow confines of their job description, they say, "That's not my job." Their union contract may well back them up. For some individuals, this is a great deal—until the job or the organization disappears. For job-based organizations, this is a problem: crucial

pieces of work do not get done or get done much too slowly and after much too much argument.

2. Jobs and job-based organizational structures encourage hiring. If changing conditions create new tasks that need doing, it seems obvious to job holders that employers should create new jobs and hire people to fill them. Besides, the job of the manager is enhanced if the number of his or her reports is increased. The fact that you have divided the work up into jobs encourages you, in two different ways, to do some hiring. When inflation covered the rising cost structure of many organizations, that may have been a tolerable situation. But today, when value is such a market demand, unnecessary hiring must be avoided.

3. Jobs obscure the larger picture and the ultimate goals of the collective effort. People do things that do not contribute or perhaps take actions that actually undermine the larger effort, but they justify them by arguing, "I'm just doing my job." Many once reasonable but now unnecessary (or even detrimental) activities continue because they are part of somebody's job. Needless to say, it is hard for people to accept that "doing their job" may actually be diminishing the organization's effectiveness.

4. Finally, in an increasingly rootless society, people's jobs have come to be a major source of their identities. Ask people who they are and they say, "I am a machinist (eligibility worker/sales manager/R&D executive/pediatric nurse/real estate broker)." It is hardly surprising that such people will view anything that threatens their jobs as a threat to their very existence. In times of family fragmentation, community breakdown, and general transience, people hold on to their jobs desperately. That has long been true in industrialized societies, and when jobs were more secure it caused relatively little difficulty. But today, the job identity is much too fragile a peg on which to hang a healthy life. Most of us resist any effort at organizational change that threatens those jobs—even when it may be necessary to preserve employment in the organization.

For these reasons, jobs are dysfunctional in all but the slowest-moving organizations today. They are an old way of getting work done that does not fit the realities of the new economy but fits the expectations of many workers all too well. Because the prospect of a workplace in which jobs matter less and less is almost inconceivable to most workers, employers don't want to talk about what is really happening. (It will frighten people too much, they argue.) In fairness, it must be admitted that most employers do not themselves understand what is really happening. But their actions contribute to dejobbing just as surely as if they were part of a well-thought-out strategy.

FOCUS YOUR ENERGIES ON WHATEVER NEEDS DOING

In this workplace that is being steadily dejobbed, it isn't enough any longer to find a "growing industry" or a "profession with a future" or a "trade that is going to expand." Instead, you need to focus your efforts on becoming a different kind of worker. To take advantage of the opportunities that exist today and will increase tomorrow, you need to rebuild your career around a strategy for finding the work that needs doing in order to provide what a customer wants or enhance a client's ability to provide what his or her customer wants.

It is a good idea to start here: security no longer resides in the job (*any* job). It resides in your ability to add value to what some organization does or, more specifically, to add value to what the organization's customer gets for his or her buck. This enhanced value may be added directly if you interface with the customer yourself. It may come once removed if you can improve the product or service that the customer receives. Or it may come twice removed if you provide something that enhances a client's ability to deliver something of value to his or her customer.

The skills you need to develop for this value-adding task aren't the old job-based skills, or even those esoteric computer skills you wish you had. For the most part, they are the skills that enable you to find out what needs to be done, adapt your resources to that task, and present yourself as the answer to someone's need. They are actually skills that are less often associated with being a good employee than they are with being a successful small-business operator. That is why Part III of this book talks about how to run "You & Co.," the "little business" that will power your career.

The point I want to make here is that you'll be running your career as a business regardless of whether you are an employee for your present employer, an employee for a new employer, or an independent worker who contracts to do projects for one employer or the other. Robert Schaen, the former controller of the regional phone company, Ameritech, has put it this way:

> *The days of the mammoth corporations are coming to an end. People are going to have to create their own lives, their own careers and their own successes. Some people may go kicking and screaming into the new world, but there is only one message there: You're now in business for yourself.*

Schaen has taken his own advice literally, having become a publisher of children's books, but you don't literally have to go into business for yourself to work in this new way.

To See the Future, Look at the Movies

To appreciate the range of possibilities that exist, take a look at an industry that has gone further than most industries in dejobbing: the movie business. If you had been an actor, a camera operator, a makeup specialist, or a director back in the 1940s, the chances are that you would have been an employee. Movies back then were made by big corporations (MGM, 20th Century Fox, Warner Brothers), and if you wanted to work in that business you had little choice but to get yourself hired by a big studio.

But in the next generation the movie business came apart. The big studios were slowly "unbundled" into many smaller, narrower operations. Some became independent film companies, most of which were little more than a few key people with their immediate support staff. Television emerged as a new kind of competition for the movies, and people started up hundreds of little technical support businesses (lighting, special effects, sound, costumes, and film crew logistics). Yesterday's employee at a big company became today's small-business operator, as big projects were undertaken by ad hoc clusters of small firms under the direction of an independent producer.

I first crossed paths with this world through the computer consultant my own small business was using. He and his wife had broken away from the big computer company they used to work for to set up the classic little service company, helping technologically unsophisticated people like me harness the new computer power that was becoming available. Early in his work with my firm he warned us that he might have to discontinue our business relationship for a while if a well-known producer got funding for a new film.

I didn't quite follow the connection, so he explained that his job for his old computer employer had been in finance, but that his avocation had always been film. Early in his career as an independent businessperson, he had been hired by the producer in question to set up and administer the bookkeeping for a film. He loved it and the producer liked his work, so they had repeated the arrangement periodically over the next few years. Now, the producer had come to him for help once again. Our consultant said that he would find us another computer consultant if necessary and work with his replacement for a little while to bring him or her up to speed on our project. He'd also come back when the film was finished if we wished. And so it turned out; he had to leave. He handled the changeover very professionally, we liked his replacement, and both the movie producer and we got done the work that needed doing.

Such a worker—independent and moving from one client organization to another on the basis of need and opportunity—is one possible model for the dejobbed worker. Another is the person who wishes to stay with one employer but nevertheless runs his or her career as though operating in the external marketplace. 3M is a company that has encouraged that kind of worker. Len Royer, the former head of the 3M unit where the ubiquitous Post-Its were developed, has described this kind of dejobbed workplace thus:

> *No one says "We'll help you." If you have an idea, you form your little ad-hoc group—it may be two people. You don't have top management supporting you. You take your idea to where you bake the bread and let the aroma filter out and see how they respond. If they don't bother to come and eat your bread, you throw it out and feed it to the birds. But if they like it, you'll know.*

You may be an *employee* at 3M, but the way you work is certainly more like being in business for yourself than like having an old-fashioned job.

TO SEE THE FUTURE, LOOK AT NEW INDUSTRIES

The companies that are capitalizing on the opportunities offered by today's fast-moving markets depend on employees who operate quite independently. A software design engineer at Microsoft captured the spirit at many cutting-edge companies when she told an interviewer, "You won't last at Microsoft if your job is just a job." Employees there have no regular hours, but are under constant pressure to deliver promised output on time and at a high level of quality. Because people manage themselves like independent businesspeople rather than like standardized workers, there are no pre-established career paths within the company. This means, in the words of a human resources manager at the company, that

> *if people want to change functions or they want to go get different experiences, that's not frowned on at all. There's a lot of movement internally and laterally. . . . Employees drive their own development, and we need to design all of our management and our training programs to support, augment and facilitate that development. . . . [You] start from the person's goals—the long term goals—and then fit in your short term tactical methods for augmenting those [goals].*

These people are "employees," but the spirit of their work is very independent. They handle their careers as though they were independent professionals setting and following individual business plans.

Dejobbed work is the dominant mode of activity at Microsoft, CNN, Intel, Condé Nast Publications, EDS, Andersen Consulting, and many other successful companies. It is also quite evident at hundreds of less famous companies. What does the future hold? More of the same, probably. As Peter Schwartz, the former head of Planning at Royal Dutch Shell who developed the influential scenario-based planning process has said recently,

> *It's plausible to me that in 10 years we will not see today's multinationals but, rather, large "umbrella" organizations that act as hosts for many small companies that come together for brief periods to do short-term but big projects—for example, the production of a new car. But the umbrella organization may not be an enduring organization in the way, say, GM has been.*

I suspect that GM will make this shift fairly late in the process, and that jobs may last there long after they have disappeared elsewhere. But that also may not be so. Consider GM's push to outsource more of its auto components and the battles it has had with its unions over that effort. When a bureaucracy cannot get its job-minded workers to change, it has the trump card of outsourcing. No less a bureaucracy than the Department of Inland Revenue in the United Kingdom (the equivalent of the Internal Revenue Service in the United States) gave up trying to get its information technology workers to change and outsourced them en masse to EDS.

HOW TO DEAL WITH DEJOBBING

When I began to speak and write about the disappearance of jobs, I was surprised by two aspects of the reaction I got. The first was that my audience split down the middle:

- One side said that what I was saying was crazy and would never happen.
- The other side said that what I was saying was obvious and that to a large extent it had already happened.

I realized what this split signified during a debriefing session that followed a pilot seminar based on these ideas that I ran at a large telephone company. After several participants had argued on both sides of the question, one manager had the last word by commenting, "I think that this program is somewhat ahead of its time, *and* that we needed it a year ago." Situationally, these changes are washing the ground out from under the feet of today's workers, but emotionally, most workers aren't ready to deal with the implications of their plight. That is a dangerous situation, for they are losing precious time that ought to be spent rebuilding their careers. One could wish that such workers had assistance from corporations, government programs, unions, educational institutions, and nonprofit agencies. But they do not. At the moment, workers are largely on their own. That is the reason that this workbook is being written.

The second surprise was how differently different listeners heard what I was saying. Many people thought that I was praising the move toward dejobbing—that I was saying that the dejobbed organizations and the careers that they encouraged were "better" than their job-based counterparts, that dejobbing was a "good thing," and that people and companies would be better off without jobs than they had been with them.

That isn't what I mean at all. I don't think that dejobbing is a good thing—or a bad thing. It just *is*. What I am saying is that big changes have taken place and that people need to shift their career thinking accordingly. To argue *in favor* of these changes would be like arguing in favor of the weather. These changes, like the weather, are part of the reality we live with. They are driven by forces that do not bend to our wishes. Like the weather, these forces influence our actions, making some things wise and other things foolish. If it is raining, we had probably better forget the picnic, no matter how much we would prefer to eat outside. If it is freezing, the swimming will have to wait.

I am talking about actual (not hypothetical) changes that have already taken place. This isn't some vague "futurism." These changes are transforming the workplace just as surely as the machinery of industrialism and the economics of capitalism began to do two hundred years ago. At that time, Adam Smith wrote *The Wealth of Nations* to demonstrate the efficacy of "the division of labor," which is the underpinning of the industrialized job world. When he published the book in 1776, it was hard to believe that people's lives would be so profoundly changed by work arrangements that then affected only a minority of British workers and hardly any workers in other countries.

Another of Smith's insights that was just as significant as the division of labor was the recognition that when the system by which work is done changes, people's roles, values, sense of identity, and social arrangements must change too. To paraphrase a slogan from Bill Clinton's 1992 presidential election campaign, it was Adam Smith who realized, "It's the means of production, stupid!" All those things changed with industrialism, and they are changing again with the postindustrial shifts we have chronicled above.

THE PAIN OF CHANGE

The coming of industrialism caused immense pain, and its passing will do the same. The great philosopher Alfred North Whitehead rightly noted that "it is the first step in sociological wisdom to recognize that the major advances in civilization are processes which all but wreck the societies in which they occur." While we are drawing from the wisdom of great minds, let's add the comment of Henry Thomas Buckle, the English historian, whose *History of Civilization* was the most widely read survey of its day:

> *Every new truth which has ever been propounded has, for a time caused mischief; it has produced discomfort, and often unhappiness; sometimes disturbing social and religious arrangements, and sometimes merely by disruption of old and cherished association of thoughts. It is only after a certain interval, and when the framework of affairs has adjusted itself to the new truth, that its good effects preponderate; . . . but at the outset there is always harm. And if the truth is very great as well as very new, the harm is serious.*

So, far from having too optimistic a view of dejobbing, I fear its far-reaching effects and am determined to spend the rest of my own career helping people to prepare themselves for it.

TAKING STOCK OF YOUR OWN READINESS

The conclusion of this chapter will be a little inventory of your own attitudes and assumptions, consisting of statements that are often made about the contemporary employment situation. It isn't a quiz, and the goal is not to be right or to get a high score. The goal is to highlight topics that you need to think about and come to terms with.

Read each statement and think for a moment about how it corresponds to your assumptions. Place a check beside it if you've heard this statement before seeing this book and you agree with it. Place a check-plus if you've actually said something like this yourself. And place a check-minus if you've never heard anyone say anything like this, or if you disagreed when someone did say it. Then proceed to the commentary that follows this list.

___ 1. Good jobs are taking longer to "come back" after this recent recession, but (with time and good public policy) they will.

___ 2. The main source of job loss in this country has been the lower cost of labor in other countries.

___ 3. All of this is just the latest chapter in our work being taken over by machines.

___ 4. Information technology is a "solvent" that is causing jobs to vanish.

___ 5. "Outsourcing" will pass. Besides, they only outsource peripheral functions; you can't outsource the basic tasks that an organization relies on.

___ 6. These job cuts are the product of corporate greed. If companies weren't so selfish, they'd hire more workers and pay them good wages and salaries.

___ 7. In today's unstable job market, you're relatively safe if you have a lot of schooling—especially if you have an advanced degree.

___ 8. The "contingent" workforce now performs at least 25 percent of the work being done in America.

___ 9. The disappearance of jobs in America is different from that in Japan and continental Europe, both because "lifetime employment" exists in those places and because they have much more generous safety nets than we have.

___10. Fast-moving companies are largely doing away with jobs—implicitly, if not explicitly.

___11. If you have good computer skills, job security is still possible.

___12. Your most secure employment in the long term is going to be a union-protected job in a *Fortune* 500 company.

___13. The "job" is a historical phenomenon, and as such it has a limited life expectancy.

___14. The job-based workforce is what created the middle class, and the disappearance of jobs is an enormous step backwards.

___15. The heart of any viable job search plan today is to foresee which fields are going to grow in the coming years and prepare yourself to get a job in one of them.

Now here are my comments on each of these statements, based on what I've seen and heard and read while working in this field.

1. **Jobs are taking longer to "come back" after this recent recession, but (with time and good public policy) they will.** This is a widely held assumption, especially in public policy circles. It confuses *work* with *jobs* and underestimates how much work has changed from the period when jobs dominated the workplace.

2. **The main source of job loss in this country has been the lower cost of labor in other countries.** This is a superficial and misleading explanation for what is going on. ("All we need to do is to keep out all this low-cost stuff made in low-wage countries.") There are two problems with this interpretation:

   a. As consumers, we're voting in favor of those goods every day. To replace them with costlier homemade goods represents a lifestyle hit that most Americans would hate.

   b. Even if we kept out that "foreign" stuff (there's a hidden agenda there too), we'd find the same erosion of jobs at big traditional companies as they lost out to smaller, dejobbed domestic companies.

3. **All of this is just the latest chapter in our work being taken over by machines.** Technology is a cause—no doubt about that. But this time it's information technology; the change is not just the quantitative shift of a guy on a tractor doing ten times the work of a guy behind a horse. The nature of the work has changed. It still needs to be done—we aren't going to run out of work—but it can't be divided up effectively into jobs.

4. **Information technology is a "solvent" that is causing jobs to vanish.** This is true. The details are in the chapter and can be summed up in the statement that info-tech endows the single worker with many of the benefits of a larger, tightly integrated organization—and that it accelerates the pace of change enormously.

5. **"Outsourcing" will pass. Besides, they only outsource peripheral functions; you can't outsource the basic tasks that an organization relies on.** It's unlikely that something that increases flexibility, usually cuts costs, and often also enhances quality is only a fad. And it is flat-out wrong to assume that only the lesser functions can be done outside the company. If that were so, Lotus wouldn't have de-

veloped its best-selling *Notes* and Boston Brewing wouldn't be able to produce its prizewinning Samuel Adams Beer. The former was developed by a little start-up firm run by a former Lotus employee, Ray Ozzie, and the latter is brewed entirely by other breweries according to Boston Brewing's specifications.

6. **These job cuts are the product of corporate greed. If companies weren't so selfish, they'd hire more workers and pay them good wages and salaries.** Yes, there's a lot of greed in organizations today—at every level. But if you confiscated the CEO's excessive package and divided it up among the whole workforce, it wouldn't make a big difference in the workers' pay. It's not greed but rather the need for flexibility and responsiveness that is driving most companies away from full-time, long-term jobs.

7. **In today's unstable job market, you're relatively safe if you have a lot of schooling—especially if you have an advanced degree.** This assumption is not only wrong but dangerous. It encourages people not to change their outlook—just to pay a lot of money for further schooling. The fact is that degrees are becoming so common that they matter less than they used to—at least at companies where the focus is not on formal qualifications but on the ability to turn out work. And those are the companies that are leaving the sorry-but-you-don't-have-a-master's organizations in the dust.

8. **The "contingent" workforce now does about 25 percent of the work being done in America.** If you added up the total number of temps, contractors, part-timers, and consultants, the figure would indeed be large. But that's counting trees and missing the forest. The forest is that we're *all* contingent workers today: today's employment is contingent on the worker's ability to deliver value. Oh, I know that there are bureaucracies and contract-guaranteed work situations where you don't have to deliver. But they're disappearing, and besides, do you want to build your career on ground that is slipping into the sea?

9. **The disappearance of jobs in America is very different from that in Japan and continental Europe, both because "lifetime employment" exists in those places and because they have much more generous safety nets than we have.** It's true that cultural differences are

very important in how people are treated at work. But the forces of what we are calling dejobbing are everywhere. Besides, lifetime employment (which never was what those words say) is being undermined everywhere. Who would imagine that my first book on these changes, *JobShift,* would have been translated into Japanese? It was, and it was also published in Brazil, Germany, Great Britain, Australia, Korea, France, Taiwan, Greece, the Netherlands, and Indonesia. These changes are happening worldwide.

10. **Fast-moving companies are largely doing away with jobs—implicitly, if not explicitly.** Yup. Not that they don't hire people and give them paychecks and seat them at offices with a nameplate on the door. No, it's simply that the notion of security coming with "having a job" and "doing your job faithfully" and the idea that what you do can even be captured in a "job description"—concepts that used to be the heart and soul of the job world—are gone forever.

11. **If you have good computer skills, job security is still possible.** There's no doubt that a familiarity with computers is a plus today, but if all you needed to have job security were computer skills, then there wouldn't have been all those layoffs at IBM, Apple, and hundreds of smaller fish in the electronic tank. Sorry for the Johnny-one-note routine, but there's no shortcut to adding value. In fact, many of the clearest paths to adding value have little to do with booting up.

12. **Your most secure employment in the long term is going to be a union-protected job in a *Fortune* 500 company.** Wow, have you been spelunking these last few years? The *Fortune* 500—or at least the more traditional companies in the group—are indeed the heartland of the job-world, but their workforces have been shrinking steadily for a dozen years. And given the folks who've been left behind on cross-trained, cross-functional teams (no job descriptions there!) that include external consultants and ex-employees who return as contract hires, dejobbing is reaching right into Job City.

13. **The "job" is a historical phenomenon, and as such it has a limited life expectancy.** This is true, and it's something that we need to understand. So much of our thinking is job-based! We have to recognize that the job is not part of God's creation. It was produced by a

particular kind of work that needed to be done, and with that kind
of work no longer dominant, organizations are hiring, paying, and
organizing people to get work done in ways that have little to do
with "jobs."

14. **The job-based workforce is what created the middle class, and the
disappearance of jobs is an enormous step backwards.** As you
might guess, I don't see this development as a "step backwards" (or
forwards, for that matter). But this statement is not all wrong. Jobs
did build the middle class, and the disappearance of jobs is going to
have a big, though presently unforeseeable, impact on social sta-
tuses and arrangements. The mortgages that the middle class used
to buy houses were based on regular, predictable salaries. If those
give way to something more unpredictable, what happens to home
ownership? Good question! This book doesn't aim to explain what's
coming next in home ownership, just how you can ensure your own
income and fulfilling work.

15. **The heart of any viable job search plan today is to foresee which
fields are going to grow in the coming years and prepare yourself to
get a job in one of them.** By this time you know what I'm going to
say. I'm going to say that the roadside is littered with people who
(a) tried to guess tomorrow's hot field, and (b) *did* guess right, but
went after job security and got tossed out when the truck turned a
corner. This is going to get tiresome, but one more time: *forget jobs;
look for the work that needs doing!* That work exists in businesses that
are in "nonhot" fields too. So *forget jobs* and fields . . . and you'll
find that (yes, Virginia) *there is work that needs doing everywhere.*

CHAPTER TWO

Finding Your Lifework Through Your D.A.T.A.

No [one] is born into the world whose work
Is not born with him.

—James Russell Lowell, "A Glance Behind the Curtain"

I always wanted to be somebody, but I should have been more specific.

—Lily Tomlin and Jane Wagner

THE INWARD FACTOR

Chapter 1 dealt with the outward half of the challenge that each of us faces in constructing a career today—the need to understand the changes that are invalidating our assumptions about work and rendering many of our plans obsolete. This chapter deals with the inward half of the challenge—the need to see and be able to present ourselves in a new way. These two needs go together, because it is the changes that force us to understand in a new way what it is that we have to offer and then invent new ways to utilize those resources.

Now career planning wasn't always this way. In the same way that yesterday's job holders could forget about the markets they worked in and the organizations they worked for, just as long as they understood their jobs and did them, they could also forget about understanding them-

27

selves. Jobs minimized the differences between individual workers. What you or I wanted was irrelevant. We each had talents we'd never used, but that didn't matter because no one really believed that the average job gave you a chance to express yourself. The fact that we were really temperamentally better suited to a kind of work other than what we did was . . . well, one of those unfortunate things that happen in the world of work. Life wasn't fair, and work especially wasn't fair. Our employers were just paying us for carrying out some clearly specified activities, and as long as we could and did carry them out, we got our pay. Jobs were slots, boxes, pigeonholes. It was nice when they fit, but the company wasn't paying us for self-expression. Jobs demanded performance in a script that was already written.

But now it's different. In the dejobbed world we're working without scripts, adding value in whatever way we can to what the customer gets from dealing with the organization. It's not a nine-to-five-and-then-forget-it world anymore, either. With everyone in competition with someone, there is always another person who'd love to take over your tasks and would be willing to put in an extra hour on them. Today's workers may not give that mythical 110 percent, but they find to their dismay that they're being measured by that standard.

This is a world in which people had better be doing whatever they do best, whatever they are really motivated to do, whatever most suits them temperamentally, and whatever makes best use of such assets as they happen to have. In this new workplace organizations pay for results, and we're more like little companies selling products than employees doing jobs: it's You & Co. again. If our little companies lack the resources to create and deliver their products, they won't get the business next time. Our clients are paying for benefits received, not tasks done.

The inner aspect of the new work situation is that each of us has some unique combination of motivation, capability, style, and incidental advantages that represents the work that fits us, the work that we were made for, our lifework. In the old job world this was equally true, but it was essentially irrelevant since jobs were boxes and we trimmed ourselves to fit them. Besides, after that first job got us started, many of us found ourselves on a vocational moving sidewalk that had a predetermined destination. Hopes, preferences, and talents were pretty things, but not very practical.

In the dejobbed world, the truth that each of us has an inherent lifework is suddenly rich with meaning. Nothing less than finding what you were meant to be and do will give you the motivation and the capability that today's work world demands. Identifying your lifework is no longer an escapist fantasy. It is a condition for being successful. You now have to discover your lifework if you are to have a chance of creating a satisfactory and satisfying work life.

THE OLD QUALIFICATIONS

When there were jobs to be filled, there were all those *qualifications:* a degree or certificate, so many years of experience, and references from somebody whose position carried some weight. If you lacked those things, you were stuck. You'd think that with the scarcity of good jobs today, the Qualification Derby would be an even tougher race. And so it is—where *jobs* are involved. Job applicants outnumber job openings ten to one, twenty to one, sometimes even one hundred to one. But where people find the work that needs doing and show that they have the resources to get it done, the Qualification Derby is a very different race. Where it is "work to be done" and not a "job to be filled," there is no line of applicants. Clients with unmet needs aren't poring over résumés; they are worrying about how to get their problems solved. And the questions they are asking aren't, "Do you have a master's degree?" or "What is your job history?" They are, "What would you do to solve this problem?" and "How do I know that you can do it?"

Take the matter of education. Although some traditional companies still require a college degree for an entry-level job, one-fifth of the *Forbes* 200 Best Small Companies are run by people who did not go beyond high school. Microsoft and Oracle have done pretty well under their "unqualified" CEOs: neither Bill Gates nor Larry Ellison graduated from college.

Traditional companies built their hiring around what can be called the Three Es: Education, Experience, and Endorsements. It is remarkable how many companies—and they include today's market leaders—have abandoned the Three Es in favor of a very different way of assessing who's qualified to do the necessary work.

Education

Perhaps it's that today's knowledge has such a short shelf life and techniques learned today are abandoned tomorrow; or perhaps, as Lewis Perelman has argued in *School's Out,* it's that conventional education no longer guarantees learning and the best learning currently takes place outside educational institutions. Or perhaps it's that grades and certificates simply measure the abilities to get through an academic program. Or maybe it's that education is so common today that it no longer signifies what it once did. Whatever the reason, education means less today than it ever has. Everyone needs a basic education, but a college diploma or even a graduate degree no longer opens the door to success. We hear stories about cab drivers with Ph.D.'s and waitresses with master's degrees, and we say, "Man, it's a jungle out there!" What we ought to be saying is that education has lost its power to get you hired. A relatively unquestioned key to the job world, an advanced education is becoming less and less able to guarantee anything in the dejobbed world.

Experience

Experience is a tricky word. When it means that a person can do a task because he or she has done it before, "experience" can be useful. I want my surgeon to have *experience*. I want the pilot on my transcontinental airliner to have *experience*. But do I want to require everyone I hire to have *experience?* No, I don't think so. Nordstrom doesn't require salespeople to have experience. The company finds that a sales job elsewhere simply teaches a worker bad habits. (I'll talk about what Nordstrom *does* require later, because it shows the extent to which dejobbing has changed the hiring process.) Henry Bessemer, whose revolutionary discovery made modern steelmaking possible, wrote of his breakthrough, "I had an immense advantage over many others dealing with the problem inasmuch as I had no fixed ideas derived from long-established practice to control and bias my mind, and did not suffer from the general belief that whatever is, is right." Do modern companies want *experience?* Often they don't—in practice—although their words may make it sound otherwise. Experience is a particularly dubious qualification during periods of radical and frequent change—the very conditions that are dejobbing our organizations.

Endorsements

Well, sometimes. Certainly, if we can talk to someone who knows the candidate well . . . and if the person is skilled at evaluation . . . and if the person will be frank . . . and if the person will take the time to be specific . . . then hearing from someone who knows the candidate's work can be helpful. But more often than not, "letters of recommendation" today consist of vague statements that no one can sue the writer for, evaluations that consistently overrate candidates, and recommendations that show little understanding of the tasks the new employee will be expected to do.

Education, experience, and endorsements: those were the Three Es that formed the basis of job requisitions and job applications alike. They had little enough to do with who you really were or what you could really do, but they were what you built your résumé on. The Three Es were so unquestioned that we even used them to try to determine what we could do to make a living. They are not, however, what you need to find work for You & Co. today.

THE NEW QUALIFICATIONS: YOUR D.A.T.A.

Practices change faster than concepts do. The old "reality" hangs around long after it ceases to explain how people are actually behaving. It's that way with hiring. As I studied who was actually getting hired and why, I came up with the acronym D.A.T.A. to signify the key elements of the process as it was really being practiced. If you want to position yourself not as a job applicant but as the best way to get something done, the best way to get a problem solved, or the best way to capitalize on a ripe opportunity, build your case on your D.A.T.A.

D = Desire

Show (don't say, *show*) that you desire the task more than the other people who are interested in it. Organizations are starting to realize that motivation is the keystone of success. Silicon Graphics recently hired some technical staff, and a *Wall Street Journal* description of their methods concluded that they passed over people with better technical qualifications in favor of people who had demonstrated by their actions that they desired the position more.

It's easy to forget about Desire or to rely on just talking about it. It used not to matter much. Your parents and teachers told you that they didn't care what your desires were, remember? It wasn't what you *wanted* but what you *had* to do. Jobs were all about "have to do." The well-qualified candidates used to be the people who had repressed their desires to the point where these no longer got in the way of doing their jobs. No wonder people didn't think much about what they desired—except when they daydreamed about a fantasy job at a perfect company.

The point is that the situation has changed. You just won't be able to do the kind of high-quality work that today's employer expects unless you are doing what you really desire to be doing. It's as simple as that!

This isn't to say that if your present job doesn't qualify as desirable, you ought to walk in tomorrow and resign. Today's job may be the best staging area that you could possibly have for planning the next leg of your career journey. Whether you presently have such a job or not, the first element in your plan for a job-free career is to determine what it is that you really *desire* at this point in your life.

A = Abilities

Do you have what it'll take to get the work done, to accomplish the task, to solve the problem? That's unlikely to be a question that can be answered with a list of the jobs you have held. An increasing number of organizations are bypassing job histories and asking you to describe how you solved a problem or achieved a result in the past. Some even set up a real-time version of the tasks you'll face if they hire you. *Forbes* magazine's offshoot, *FYI,* was recently looking for an editorial assistant. They seated fourteen applicants in a room and announced that they were holding an "audition" for the position. The audition was a timed treasure hunt, in which each applicant was given a list of items to find, including

- the best price in New York for the first edition of an Evelyn Waugh novel
- the best charter options in the Caribbean for a particular kind of sailboat
- unlisted home phone numbers of several celebrities

These were the kinds of things that an editorial assistant at *FYI* might be asked to find later, so they wanted to discover at the start who had the *ability* to accomplish such tasks. The winner of the treasure hunt was hired.

Your abilities aren't technical skills, although they include (if you have it) the ability to learn technical skills quickly. They are qualities that you have used before, qualities that are probably the basis of most of the things you've ever been good at and of most of your accomplishments. They aren't the result of training, and in fact most of them were probably evident to insightful people when you were in grade school.

Abilities aren't just used in their original form. They get "recycled" into new forms throughout a person's career. Jim McCann, who is the head of Teleway and is best known as the developer of the worldwide flower delivery service 800-FLOWERS, started his career as a social worker. An interviewer asked him if there were any carryovers from the old field to the new one. Sure, said McCann:

> *When you're a social worker, you have to have entrepreneurial skills and fight the bureaucracy. It really is a wrestling match. . . . You [also] have to be good at balancing and getting different things to go in the same direction or the common good. That's the same thing we're trying to do in business, right? You have to get different kinds of forces to come together to achieve the vision you have and to get other people to buy into that vision.*

I'll bet that these abilities were pretty clear even when McCann was in grammar school.

Lest you think, after all the talk in Chapter 1 about high-tech companies and the wired workplace, that your abilities need to be something out of *Star Wars,* let me list the "Ten Basic Skills for the Workplace" as they were recently summarized in the journal of the American Society for Training and Development:

1. reading
2. writing
3. computing
4. speaking
5. listening
6. solving problems
7. managing oneself

8. knowing how to learn
9. working as part of a team
10. leading others

My point isn't that your skills couldn't be improved. It may turn out that you ought to start enhancing some of them right away. My point is that you already have the basic abilities that you need. It isn't as though you had to dash out and start learning Lithuanian or computer programming.

T = Temperament

Even in organizations where technical training is important, so is temperament. Samuel Metters, the CEO of a successful engineering firm outside Washington, D.C., recently told an interviewer that his employees were technically competent but that for a long time Metters Industries got only initial contracts to do government work. They kept losing the follow-on work to other firms. He recalled:

> *I remember presenting a proposal to a government agency, and watching my employees ram our ideas down the representative's throat. If the government had to decide between Metters Industries and a company with equal technical resources, the decision makers would choose the other company because we didn't understand how to treat people. . . . Now I look for candidates who have . . . a warm side to their personality. I just hired a man whose ratio of social skills to technical skills is about 70 to 30. We're finally beginning to win those follow-up contracts.*

Note that although Metters talks about "social *skills*," he is not using training but hiring to deal with the problem. He is looking for people with a different temperament ("a warm side to their personality") rather than for people with what we usually mean by "a skill."

Many successful companies recognize temperament as critical to success. You hear a lot about Nordstrom's incredible customer service, and you might imagine that the retailer has some sophisticated training program to build that capability in its salespeople. But no, Nordstrom does relatively little customer service training. A representative chalks up the company's service excellence to the fact that it "hires new employees primarily on the basis of their *friendliness*." A consultant who has worked with the retailer for a long time echoes this assessment: "A long tradition at Nordstrom is hiring nice people who like people and have been brought up to have good manners." It makes you wonder: how much training is needed simply because companies didn't hire people with the appropriate temperament in the first place?

A = Assets

When you have tallied up the varying degrees of Desire, the Abilities, and the underlying Temperaments of half a dozen candidates, one hitherto unnamed factor may still put one or two ahead of the rest. That is their Assets—characteristics, experiences, areas of expertise, or possessions that give them an advantage over their rivals. These Assets are almost never universal ones, but rather advantages in relation to the demands of the work to be done.

Here are some examples. As you read them, remember that the combination of characteristics and situations means that there are literally millions of things that might be Assets:

- Having grown up in a family where Spanish, Cambodian, or Russian was spoken could be an Asset if an organization was expanding its overseas work.
- Having minored in geology could be an Asset if one's new client was a mining or drilling company.
- Having spent a summer straightening out the filing system in your uncle's law office could be an Asset if you had a client that was trying to reengineer its clerical work processes.
- Having a good deal of equity in your house can be an Asset if you are considering leaving your job and starting your own business.
- Having impressive education, experience, or endorsements (the Three Es) can sometimes be an Asset. (I've gotten good mileage out of the fact that I have a Ph.D., even though it has very little relevance to what I actually do these days.)

Assets are incidental advantages that you have (if you realize that they are Assets) just because of who you are and where your life has taken you. You may need to know something about your client to realize that they are Assets, however. Let's say that you worked for three years for a company that went in and out of bankruptcy before finally collapsing completely. You may regard that as a blot on your record, but to an organization that was struggling through bankruptcy proceedings, it would be an Asset.

That's what I mean when I say that Assets depend not just on you but on the situation. They are something about you that could be an advantage in a particular situation. They may not be a "strength," and they may in fact be something that you wish you didn't have. But they can be Assets, all the same.

OTHER QUALITIES PEOPLE LOOK FOR

The more you know about yourself, the more wisely you can draw on what you have to offer, so I don't want to rule out assessing any of your qualities. But over time, I've found some widely used categories much less helpful in putting together the product that you're going to bring to your market than they may have been in the heyday of job hunting.

Take *values*. Many books on job hunting contain long lists of values, from which you are supposed to choose the ones that are most important to you. Is "security" what you need, or is it "freedom to express yourself"? (I always want to say "both.") Is "service to mankind" higher or lower on the list than "being part of a professional community"? Then there is the fact that although I would tell you that I value some things deeply (like intimate relationships), some people who know me well might disagree with my self-assessment. Ditto regarding some values that I would say that I *don't* care so much about (like "financial success"). Maybe we should give the values inventory to our friends to fill out on our behalf.

Values are certainly important in my life and yours, but they are so slippery! There are professed values and values in action. There are the values we are trying to live up to and the values that we are trying to move away from. There are values we live by at work and those we live by at home—and then there's that darned value we place on wholehearted commitment that says that we shouldn't have these value conflicts in the first place.

Values are certainly slippery. Yet my experience is that when you have factored in the things that you truly Desire, the Abilities that make some types of work much more rewarding than others, and the preferences that are inherent in your Temperament, you've covered most of the areas where values influence the question of what work is best for you. In short, values share a lot of territory with D.A.T.A. All of that notwithstanding, if values represent very important elements in the work you are looking for, then by all means use them to guide you.

The same is true of *interests*. They are used in many job-hunting systems, but I always go dead in the head when I am asked to list my interests. Sometimes I come out with one or two, and sometimes I have every interest in the book. If you do better with interests than I do, include them with your D.A.T.A. as clues to the work you can do for somebody. Just remember that what you are trying to define is the resources You & Co. bring into the marketplace, not the job you'd like to have. What we are inventorying corresponds to a country's natural resources. (Remember fifth-grade social studies?) Interests and values haven't helped me much when I've been trying to define what I have to offer, what someone would be glad to pay me for, what I can build into a product that a client will snap up like a trout rising to a mayfly.

Then there are *skills*. That is a catchall term that covers everything from Temperament (Metters Industries' "social skills" that turn out to be a "warm side to [applicants'] personalities"), Abilities (good "communication skills" would fall into this category), and technical skills acquired through training (the "skill" of using a bar coder, a CAD program, a C/T scanner), which I'd list as Assets. If you were born with whatever it is, if it is just how you're "wired," then I'd call it a matter of Temperament, not a skill. If it is a talent that you've had since you were a kid or a facility in certain kinds of situations that not everyone has, I'd call it an Ability. If it is something that you've been trained to do or something that you learned on the job, then it's what I'd call a "skill"—but, in that case, I'd list it as one of your Assets.

WE ARE ENTERING A NEW AGE OF SELF-RELIANCE

One of the reasons that the United States is coming to grips with dejobbing more directly than most other developed countries is its tradition of individualism. This tradition is not an unmixed blessing, since it leads Americans to undervalue the importance of membership in and reliance on a community. But it gives Americans something to stand on as they grapple with this new world in which organizations and institutions are coming apart. To put the matter in a paradoxical way, the American tradition is that we don't need a tradition, and American heroes have always been people who made things up as they went along.

Two scholars who surveyed nineteenth-century writing on child rearing identified one of its unifying themes as

> *the notion that a youngster must be able independently to go out into the urban world, to capitalize on such opportunities as it may present, to carve out a life for himself which, in a rapidly changing society, may well require different tasks to be performed than were required of his parents.*

In contrasting the past with the present, we have tended to imagine it as more stable and less atomistic than it was. In his study of the age of Andrew Jackson, Marvin Meyers wrote, "The central economic figure is . . . the speculative enterpriser who scents distant opportunities and borrows or invents the means for grasping them."

Child-rearing practices and economic forces form the backdrop to that age's most respected writer, Ralph Waldo Emerson, whose most popular piece is (not coincidentally) called "Self-Reliance." Here is a passage that has found its way into countless literature texts:

> *There is a time in every man's* [sic!] *education when he arrives at the conviction that . . . imitation is suicide; that he must take himself for better or worse as his portion; that though the wide universe is full of good, no kernel of nourishing corn can come to him but through his toil bestowed on that plot of ground which is given to him to till. The power which resides in him is new in nature, and none but he knows what that is which he can do, nor does he know until he has tried. . . . Trust thyself: every heart vibrates to that iron string.*

Trust yourself. That message has been framed in a thousand different ways, but whatever its context it remains a peculiarly American message.

It has also been a message that has been easy to misunderstand, for it seems to be a rationalization for individualistic chaos. But Emerson did not intend it that way, and if we understand that, we can still find much that is useful in it. In our present context, the Emersonian idea of self-reliance forms a philosophical frame for the necessary individualism of the dejobbed worker. For it reminds us that "imitation is suicide" in several important ways:

First, if you copy others or force yourself to copy the prescriptions laid out in job descriptions, you violate your essential uniqueness and damage your creativity. Wherever the conditions of production require little individual initiative or creativity, the gain in standardization may well justify the loss. But in today's workplace, the old virtues of "doing your job" are not enough. The heart of the D.A.T.A.-based approach to work, on the other hand, is that the best work can be done only when workers are being themselves and contributing their full energies and their own ideas.

Second, imitation is usually based on a very simplified version of the original, since the complexity of an action coming from the self is too great to comprehend and copy. Unfortunately, the widespread practice of imitating has left the impression that the copy really is the same as the original and that the differences are unimportant. This approach is similar to the way chemical fertilizer was developed, by taking organic materials, factoring them out into their main chemical components, and then combining those components into an artificial fertilizer. The results look good for a while—in both cases—but gradually the absence from the chemical fertilizer of organic matter begins to tell. The ground becomes hard, salt residues build up, the plants need more of the very fertilizer that is causing the problem, and growth weakens. So it is when you are "doing a job." At first it is interesting, but with time the repetitiveness and the artificiality of what you do builds up and you are weakened. The more "engineered" and stylized the job behaviors, the worse the problem becomes.

Third, imitation confuses the outcome with the process. You can learn a lot from watching how others approach an issue, but to copy the result of that approach produces work that is lifeless and useless. A story is currently making the rounds about the European branch of a U.S.-based computer company that turned the task of redesigning spaces in its headquarters building over to the workers themselves. The results were not only excellent, both functionally and aesthetically, but the project itself built a tremendous sense of pride and spirit in the group. The Europeans invited other branches of the company over to talk to the workers, in hopes that similar projects in self-reliant design could take place elsewhere. But they discovered to their dismay that the visitors were uninterested in the process that was the point of the whole exercise; they wanted only the *drawings of the new layout so that they could copy it!*

Fourth, imitation makes improvements and breakthrough discoveries much more unlikely. Barry Diller, the television and Hollywood executive, made this point very tellingly when he talked about his days at Paramount when it was the lowest-ranking Hollywood studio, getting to see a movie script only after the other studios had rejected it. He reflected:

> *Maybe it's a good thing not to . . . get what everyone else thinks is the best material. Maybe nobody really knows what's best. Maybe the best comes from making your own choice, on its merits not its bloodlines. Maybe it's better to be uncomfortable, and to be left alone to believe in what you can put together based on your own judgment.*

Diller was talking about how conventional wisdom produces only imitations of yesterday's success and misses completely the unusual and the new. In his case, along with the stack of third-rate imitations, *Saturday Night Fever* arrived on his desk. And it put Paramount back on the movie map.

Fifth, imitation is always playing catch-up. By the time you copy something, everyone else is copying it too and it is passé. This is true of companies, and it is equally true of the "little company" that you and your career are going to become. Even truer, because the old, big companies have some momentum, and it's going to take quite a while before their lack of creativity and flexibility bring them to a standstill. But with little You & Co., copycatting is going to make it impossible to get going in the first place. That's not a problem, though, because your D.A.T.A. is unique. You just have to find real needs—which abound in a rapidly changing marketplace—and address them in ways that enhance what your client does.

Finally, imitation costs you your soul. Really. The great Jewish theologian Martin Buber told the story of Rabbi Zosya, who was sometimes criticized for his unconventional ways. Fellow rabbis took him to task and argued that there was no need for anything but following the law of Moses and the traditions of the elders. Zosya listened to them carefully and then replied sadly, "But when I meet my God in heaven, He will not ask me, 'Why were you not Moses?' He will ask, 'Why were you not Zosya?'"

It is in this vein and in the spirit of an enlightened self-reliance that the kind of work that is replacing the job can be a rich source of individual development, of the self-realization that some traditions call *individuation*. This process of "becoming the one that you really are" is not likely to happen in the traditional job. But neither is it likely to happen in the narcissistic world of self-aggrandizement that characterizes some new, go-go companies. Individuation is likeliest to occur in the process of drawing on one's own gifts (one's D.A.T.A., if you will) and tempering them in the fire of the situations one finds in an actual workplace. That is possible today in a way that it has never been possible before.

SUMMARY

In this chapter I introduced the idea of your D.A.T.A. You shouldn't expect to know everything about putting that idea to work for you; that's what Part II of this book is for. But just to confirm your basic understanding of the D.A.T.A. idea, do this short exercise.

Read the following list of what different candidates bring to their search for work. Code each one according to the D.A.T.A. category it fits best:

D—Desire   Ab—Abilities   T—Temperament   As—Assets

At the end of the list, you'll find the way I'd match them up.

1. I have a working knowledge of Spanish.
2. I work well with children.
3. Getting my fair share is important to me.
4. I'm stubborn in the face of obstacles.
5. I want to start saving for my retirement.
6. In college I minored in economics.
7. I have advanced C++ programming skills.
8. Since my first job I've maintained a Rolodex of friends, colleagues, and acquaintances.

9. Anything involving numbers is pretty easy for me.

10. My father knows the governor of this state.

11. I'd like to be publicly recognized for what I contribute.

12. I've got to free up time to spend with my children.

13. I have a really organized streak.

14. I don't know where it came from, but somehow I usually know what's wrong with a computer when it won't work.

15. I have a photographic memory.

Here's how I'd match them up.

1. **As.** You could argue that language skills are an Ability, but Abilities tend to be characteristics that you were born with. You acquire or develop Assets.

2. **Ab.** Ease with children seems to me just the opposite—something you come by naturally, though I can see how you might have called it an Asset.

3. **D.** This entry is kind of a trick, because it doesn't include the word "desire" or "want." But your fair share *is* something you desire, isn't it? If you called this quality a Temperament, I guess I wouldn't argue.

4. **T.** OK, that's Temperament.

5. **D.** Another pretty easy one.

6. **As.** If you said Ability, your genetic makeup is pretty sophisticated.

7. **As.** Once you get the hang of D.A.T.A., you can sort things out pretty quickly.

8. **As.** We're having a run on Assets here.

9. **Ab.** Here's an Ability. Some people have it, and others don't.

10. **As.** Maybe you can turn this relationship to your advantage.

11. **D.** You could argue that seeking public recognition is part of your Temperament, I suppose, but as it is stated here, it is something you Desire.

12. **D.** Spending time with your kids is something you really want to do, right?

13. **T.** While organizational skills may be an Asset in the everyday sense, they're really part of your psychological makeup, aren't they?

14. **Ab.** OK, I know you weren't *born* with a technical instinct, but it comes naturally to you.

15. **As.** If you want to say that this is an Ability (though it's something you *have*, not something that you *do*) or even that it is part of your Temperament, I won't argue too much. However, as the author of this book, I say it's an Asset. (Pulling rank like that may say something about my Temperament, I suppose.)

PART TWO

MINING YOUR D.A.T.A.

Don't compromise yourself, honey. You're all you've got.

—JANIS JOPLIN

Showing you how to mine your D.A.T.A. is one of the goals of this book. That D.A.T.A. is the raw material that you are working with. In Part III, we will turn to the other half of the equation: the unmet needs in some market that your D.A.T.A. enables you to satisfy. But before we get into the question of your market, we need to go beyond the *idea* of D.A.T.A. and get to what that idea represents in your own case. We want to walk you through the self-assessment process, not just to describe its results.

Chapter 3 will help you identify just what you Desire at this point in your life, Chapter 4 will help you define your essential Abilities, Chapter 5 will help you describe your Temperament, and Chapter 6 will help you determine your Assets. Like chemical elements, these resources can be combined into countless "products" to respond to various unmet needs in the market that you are choosing to serve.

CHAPTER THREE

Desires: Why You Should Do What You Want

A strong passion for any object will ensure success, for the desire of the end will point out the means.

—WILLIAM HAZLITT, "ON MANNERS" (1819)

Ours is a world where people don't know what they want and are willing to go through hell to get it.

—DON MARQUIS

"I DON'T CARE WHAT *YOU* WANT!" SAYS THE BOSS

At first blush, the idea of basing your future on what you desire sounds naive. We all have long histories of being told that work *requires* you to do things, that you need to save what you *want* to do for the weekend, and that if people did just what they *felt like doing,* no work would get done.

The idea that desire is an unreliable guide goes back to your childhood, when your parents told you that it was *selfish* to do just what you desired, that you *were too young to know* what you wanted, that desires were *indulgent* (or even *sinful*), or that you only *thought* you wanted to kill your brother or to sleep with your boyfriend. Wants and desires are viewed with suspicion in our culture.

49

WHY DESIRES CREATE EFFECTIVENESS

As long as our economy's favored means of production involved fixed jobs and tightly interlocked work units, desire was too unpredictable a factor to be a basis for working. The only way that desire could figure in job selection was by luck. People's jobs weren't based on what they liked to do, except for those rare people who were paid for activities that the rest of us knew only as avocations and recreation—baseball players, singers, painters, and the like. And man, were they lucky!

I noted earlier that work activities are being unbundled into "packages" (defined by the results needed) that can be farmed out to workers who may not even be employees, and that this deconstructing of work is being done in a context of extreme competition. We also saw that in such situations, how the work is done—in terms of hours, location, or worker classification—matters far less than the fact that the workers are highly motivated to engage actively with the tasks to be done.

In that situation, the difference between workers who *desire* to do the work and those who don't can be the difference between high-quality and low-quality work, work done quickly and work that runs behind schedule, and work that finds solutions to problems and work that bogs down when problems are encountered. As the novelist Willa Cather said, "There is only one big thing—desire. And before it, when it is big, all is little."

The point is not that once you know what you desire, you'll get it. (That is one of those New Age platitudes that has left a lot of people feeling that the world owes them more than it is giving them.) The real point is that desire is too powerful a motive to leave untapped when you are seeking to capitalize on the opportunities that dejobbing creates. But desire not only represents a powerful motive force, it also enables you to create some of the other conditions for success that I have described as your D.A.T.A. The longshoreman-philosopher Eric Hoffer had that creative aspect of desire in mind when he wrote, "We are told that talent creates its own opportunities. But it sometimes seems that intense desire creates not only its own opportunities, but its own talents."

IDENTIFYING YOUR DESIRES

When you first reflect on the question of what you desire, you are likely to be overwhelmed with all the possible answers:

1. To own a 7-series BMW.
2. To spend more time with my family.
3. To lose 15 pounds.
4. To kill my boss.
5. To please my boss.
6. To please my spouse.
7. To be a movie star.
8. To finish the report in time to get home for supper.
9. To climb Mt. Everest.
10. To sleep until noon tomorrow.
11. To win ten million bucks in a lottery.
12. To do something for the homeless.
13. To work at more creative tasks.
14. To see new places.
15. To spend more time at home.

It is, to say the least, a mixed bag. The first thing to do is to list all of them, so that you can see what your desires really are. You can't do much else until you've done that. So . . .

Step One

Write down every desire that you can think of. Don't be embarrassed by silly or unattainable ones. List them all. But don't force it. When you get tired or feel that you're just making things up to lengthen the list, stop writing and set the list aside. Come back to it in a day or two. Reread your list, and add anything that occurs to you then.

Step Two

Sort the list.

Put a **D** by the items that you really, actively *desire*.

Put a **W** by the items that are simply *wishes*.

What's the difference? Well, the items about becoming a movie star, climbing Mt. Everest, and killing your boss are *wishes*—for most of us, anyway, although for an actor, a mountain climber, and a vengeful sociopath (respectively), they might be *desires*. A *wish* is something that you'd like to happen, although you aren't ready to do what it would take to create the result. As the critic Alexander Woollcott once said, "Many of us spend half our time wishing for things we could have if we didn't spend half our time wishing."

A *desire* is different. You may never have seriously looked at your desire. You may even be afraid to look at your desire, because it's something that's a little embarrassing to admit or it looks as if achieving it would take a huge effort—maybe enough to mess up your life, at least as it exists now. But as you reflect on what you desire, you start saying to yourself, "I really have to admit that I do want that one!"

For example, you may have written, "To do stand-up comedy." That's just a wish, you might tell yourself—it's just too outlandish for a person in a regular job to start telling jokes for a living. But you've been going to comedy clubs for years. You've read books by your favorite comedians, you've scribbled down a few jokes of your own, you may once even have circled a class in comedy in an adult-ed catalogue. Those are clues that being a stand-up comedian really is one of your desires. It's probably not time for an immediate career change, but move it to your desires list.

You may not know how to realize a desire yet, but it represents something that you would pursue if you knew how to do so. You don't just wish the good fairy would come along and tap you on the head with her wand. You really want to make it happen somehow, if you can. Desires are the prelude to life-changing undertakings. As the poet Audre Lorde said, "Our visions begin with our desires."

Step Three

Copy your desires into a single list (**D**), clustering any that look as though they belong together. For instance, "to drive a convertible" and "to live in a bigger apartment" might fit together. As you do that, you may recognize underlying desires, such as, in line with the previous examples, "to enjoy more luxuries." Your specific desires are like outcroppings of these deeper, more fundamental desires. Add these more basic desires at the end of your list, and put a star by them to remind yourself of their added weight. Also star any other items on your list that feel particularly significant or urgent to you.

Step Four

Now turn to the wish list (**W**)—the original list, minus the desires. Consider the items one by one, and ask yourself what desire (if any) underpins each wish. Becoming a movie star, for instance: what do you want that makes movie stardom attractive?

- Is it fame?
- Is it tons of money?
- Is it being admired by millions of people?
- Is it getting dates just by snapping your fingers?
- Is it going to Hollywood parties and knowing famous people?
- Is it having a chance to express yourself in an art form?
- Is it a way to explore other identities?
- Or is it something else?

When you figure out whatever your answer is, think about it for a while. Ask yourself why you'd feel attracted to that. Is it a real desire, or is it just a wish under a wish? If it's the latter, ask again why you'd feel attracted to that. You might have to ask *why* a couple of times to get down to the solid footing of a real desire. When you get to a desire, add it to the desire list you already have.

WHAT ABOUT "NEEDS"?

You may feel that all this talk about desires and wishes is beside the point. It might, perhaps, be worth considering in some nicer, gentler lifetime, but in this one you have some demanding, heavy-duty "needs." You may have a huge mortgage, kids starting to think about college or kids who have to go into day care (or both), or a medical condition that rules out certain kinds of employment. Shouldn't you dump the desires and start inventorying your needs?

I don't think so. You can always consider these limiting factors when you have gained a clearer picture of your resources. After all, your resources are the raw material out of which a lifework is built. You need to identify that lifework first before you can adapt it to the conditions of your present life. To put it another way, no one is paying people these days for taking care of their own needs. And besides, some of your needs should have found their way into your desires: "I want to make enough money to get my daughter into that special school . . . I want to find work that lets me spend occasional periods with my sick grandmother."

There is another, perhaps even more important reason to focus on desire and not need. Desire is an active force. It is the push behind your D.A.T.A. It resides in you. It makes you initiate things. It gets you over and around barriers. It makes things happen, it attracts "luck," it keeps you moving and brings you back to the task after setbacks.

Needs, on the other hand, are based on your lacking something. They are negative. They are passive, too, for until the need—"I've run out of food"—is converted into a desire—"I want something to eat!"—it doesn't necessarily lead to action. Besides, needs always put us in a childlike position. Under our expression of a need usually lies an unstated implication that somewhere, somehow, some surrogate Mommy or Daddy ought to come along and make things right. It is easy for "I need . . ." to take on a whiny tone. It is really a plea rather than an affirmation. "I want . . ." is more solid, more likely to lead to action, and more likely to produce results.

LEARNING MORE ABOUT YOUR DESIRES

Method One

Using blank circles like those at the top of page 55, draw two pie charts:

- 1A: show the fraction of your time that you currently spend on different activities during your working hours, depicting each as a larger or smaller piece of the pie
- 1B: show the size of your work activities relative to the other activities in your life

Now draw pie charts 2A and 2B, the first the way you *want* to spend your work time and the second the way you want to be able to *apportion* work time and nonwork-related activities.

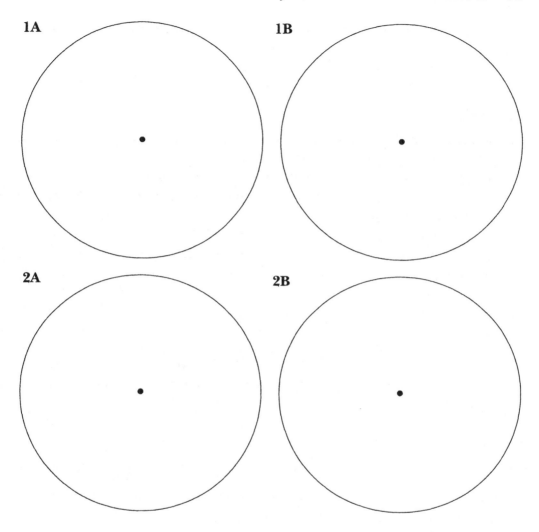

When you're finished with the four circular drawings, set them aside for a day or so. Then come back to them and imagine that they are snapshots or X rays of your situation. Study them for a while, and see what they tell you.

You might find, for example, that the parts of your work that mean something to you have become crowded down into a sliver of the day, or that you're spending a lot of your time on something that really doesn't need to be done. As you chart out the balance between work and non-work (especially if you're honest about the amount of time at home that you spend working), you may be startled to see how work is taking over your life. How do you want your time apportioned between work and non-work? And at work, what do you want to spend time doing? Having done this, do you find that you have any new desires to add to your list?

Method Two

Take a piece of paper and divide it vertically into two columns, labeled KEEP and GIVE UP, respectively, as shown on the next page.

List in the left-hand column all those aspects of your current work activities—you can include domestic, family, and volunteer responsibilities if you do not currently work for pay—that you would like to hold on to. Don't list content items like "accounting" or "answering the phone" or "cleaning." List words that describe the underlying work processes, like "controlling expenses," "helping people reach the people they want to talk to," or "bringing order into our lives." After you've done that, fill in the right-hand column with the things that you currently do that you'd happily give up.

Once again, set these lists aside for a couple of days and then come back to them with fresh eyes. If they had been written by somebody else, what would you say that these lists tell you about the desires that this person has? Add any new desires you discover to the list you are keeping.

Method Three

Study the following list of ways in which different people think of and benefit from their work. They influence the way in which people's work-related desires differ. What are the top three ways in which you relate to your work? Circle those.

1. *Work as income*—a means to an end. Do you really desire the money, or the things that the money will buy, or the way that having money makes you feel, or the feeling that comes from the fact of earning the money? If work as income is one of your top three, try to spell out the desires behind your desire for income more explicitly.

2. *Work as activity*—something that keeps you occupied and engrossed. What is it about work that produces this effect? Is it the activity itself or the escape from inactivity (or life's problems) that it provides? What is the desire underlying this one?

KEEP	GIVE UP

3. *Work as self-actualization*—a way of expressing (or even of discovering) who you are. What is it about the work that gets you in touch with yourself or reveals to you who you really are? In what way does your career represent a series of progressively developing "yous"? What is the desire that this work motive speaks to?

4. *Work as community*—a way of being together with friends and colleagues. What is it that you share? What is it that your being together with them creates? What is the sum that is greater than your parts? And what are the desires that this belonging fulfills?

5. *Work as contribution*—a way of "adding to a field of knowledge" or "improving the world" or even just "paying your dues" as a member of your society or the human race. Those phrases may not be quite right. Put into your own words what you desire to contribute through your work. And to what end do you want to contribute?

6. *Work as structure*—a way of giving a shape to your days and your years. At its simplest level, viewing work as a way to structure your life gives you a framework to hold things together. At its most complicated, the structure of work may turn it into a ritual or a formal art that has great meaning for you. Which of your desires is related to structure?

7. *Work as home base*—a way of giving you a place where you feel at home. If work serves this purpose for you, you experience getting back to work as "coming home." You are most yourself when working. Work is a place where you "belong." What desires are related to these aspects of work?

8. *Work as competence*—a way of feeling valuable, feeling OK, or of feeling on top of things, independent, expert, skillful, in control, or good at something. What desires do you associate with feelings of this sort?

9. *Work as pleasure*—an activity that is in itself enjoyable and delightful. What, specifically, is it about the activities involved in working that gives you pleasure? What increases your pleasure or diminishes it? And what desires are associated with these enjoyments?

10. *Work as game*—a competitive sport or an activity with rules where success has the air of winning a tennis match or a game of bridge.

The characteristics of this orientation are "the opponent," "winning," "keeping score," and "performing well." What desires do you have that fall into this basket?

Method Four

Think back to your earliest years of school—first, second, third grade. What did you *love* to do? What were your favorite subjects? If you had a free hour and no chores, what would you do? What books or movies, radio stations or television shows did you really like? What did you want more than anything for your birthday? What were your pastimes when you were alone? What did you most like to do with your friends on a holiday or a weekend? What did you dream of being when you grew up? And (when you have mulled those questions over) what would you say were the desires of that young person you used to be?

Method Five

Answer these questions:

1. If you were going to leave behind a personal achievement, what would it be? Or, if it is more natural to think of it this way, how would you like to be remembered?

2. What are the best times you have had in your life—however you want to define *best*—and what experiences characterize such times?

3. What are the situations in your life when you have felt most alive, most energized, most purposeful, most engaged in what you were doing?

4. What part of yourself have you not yet had the time, courage, or opportunity to live out?

5. What do you currently long for more of in your life?

6. If you were run over by a truck tomorrow, what is it that you would leave undone in your life?

7. What were you put on this earth to be and do?

OK. Now, thinking back over what went through your mind as you considered these questions, what can you say about the desires that you have at this point in your life?

Method Six

Look back over your results from all five methods of analysis above:

- The four pie charts
- The KEEP and GIVE UP lists
- The ten "work as . . ." categories
- What you desired as a child
- The seven questions

Imagine that you are a counselor looking for clues about what this person (you) really desires. Don't worry about pinning yourself down; there's no rule that says your desires can't change over time. But these exercises should have let you perceive what you really want now.

YOUR ULTIMATE DESIRES

In the light of all that you have read and written above, what are a dozen things (give or take a few) that you really want at this point in your life? These desires are going to be the content of the D of your D.A.T.A., so spell them out as clearly as you can.

CHAPTER FOUR

Abilities: What Are You Good At?

*Most [people] do violence to their natural aptitude, and thus attain
superiority in nothing.*

—BALTASAR GRACIAN, *THE ART OF WORLDLY WISDOM* (1647)

Member of the audience at a recent Washington, D.C.,
conference on Internet-based businesses:
*You [CEOs on a panel] clearly have a lot to say about [who make the best
workers]. But in all this time you've been talking, I did not hear any of you
say anything like you require a Master's degree or even mention the word
"education" at all.*

That's because education makes no difference.

—RAUL FERNANDEZ, CEO OF THE WEB-DESIGN FIRM PROXIMA, INC.

THE QUALIFICATION TRAP

There is no aspect of the modern workplace that is so intimidating to
both the entering novice and the displaced veteran as the skill levels
needed to get work done today. Before World War II a high school
diploma qualified you for most jobs. Then the GI Bill produced millions
of college graduates and raised the bar on qualification. When those post-
war graduates had children of their own, they were fed the educational
message with their formulas, and after unprecedented numbers of the
next generation went to college, we entered a world where a bachelor's
degree was no longer enough.

This educational inflationary spiral, created by the demographics of modern America, was then intensified by the knowledge revolution. Almost overnight, it seemed, it wasn't just a master's degree that you needed. You also had to possess the knowledge and the skills demanded by computers, databases, and the Internet, as well as all the business practices that those new products made possible. Especially during the recession in the early 1990s, most people knew some well-educated person who was unable to get a job because (allegedly) he or she lacked high-tech skills.

Whole generations of workers who had held good jobs, who had received good performance reviews, and who had been promoted with satisfying regularity were suddenly told that they were not needed any longer. People said sadly, "I guess I just don't have the skills they require today." Or, "Those new kids all come in with computer science degrees or MBAs with a specialization in international finance. They didn't even teach those fields when I was in school."

It is easy to see how such people imagine that this is just another ratcheting upward of the education-and-skill qualification for jobs. "Pretty soon they won't let you in without a Ph.D. in wide area networking and fluency in an Asian language!" But such views are mistaken, for the old qualifications are not being increased but rather *changed*. Raul Fernandez, the CEO quoted in the epigraph to this chapter, went on to say that the people his company hires are the ones with "good core talent." After hiring them, the company gives them a mentor who can support and guide them while they learn as they work. "Whatever know-how new hires bring with them," the CEO added, "will be obsolete in six months anyway without continuous learning."

The point cannot be overstated: Qualifications are not just rising, they are changing radically. Nowhere is this more evident than in the area of education and skill. Degrees, years of schooling, majors and minors, traditional technical or professional skills—all of these matter little. As organizations reinvent themselves, they cease to be collections of functional specialists doing things like accounting, selling, tending machinery, and designing new products. They become, instead, varying numbers and changing groupings of individual workers, clustering to accomplish tasks, carry out assignments, complete projects, and solve problems.

In Chapter 1 we saw why this is happening. In Chapter 2 we studied the way more and more of these organizations are shifting to some version of

D.A.T.A.-based hiring and, therefore, why today's prospective worker is wise to understand and learn to exploit his or her own D.A.T.A. In this chapter, we will see how this shift traps workers who are still trying to qualify for jobs on the basis of their education and their skills. We'll see how they can escape from the trap by learning how to identify their Abilities and find work that will capitalize on them.

DO YOU KNOW WHAT YOUR ABILITIES ARE?

When skills were the core of qualifications, you knew where you stood. Skills could be tested—many with simple pencil and paper exams that asked questions like the following:

If a car's motor will not start, the first thing to check is
a. the ignition switch.
b. the gas gauge.
c. the fan belt.
d. the distributor cap.

Abilities are harder to test. How do you know if a person is good with people? How do you know if a person can bring order to confused and ill-defined situations? How do you know if a person can resist automatic responses and look at a situation creatively, even under pressure? How do you know if an individual has an intuitive, sixth sense about machinery, so that the person can fix even an instrument that he or she has never seen before?

And how do you know if a person can keep on changing, letting go of old ways of doing things and learning new ways? The CEO whom I've been quoting also said that his firm's "key need is for people who show they can walk in and 'adapt' to constant change." That's pretty unambiguous, isn't it?

Well, let's look at how several very successful large organizations are finding out whether prospective hires have the basic abilities that their work will require. Their practices make it clear that the task is not easy and cannot be done quickly. Lewis Perelman reports that

Applicants at Corning's celebrated high-performance [catalytic converter] factory in Blacksburg, Virginia, are put through up to three weeks of tests, inter-

views, discussions, work simulations, and tryouts before being hired. . . . Motorola has developed a virtual factory that can give potential workers a chance to find out what working in that environment is like, whether they would want to work there, and how well they can perform.

What these organizations are doing is creating a surrogate work environment in which the prospective worker will be able to demonstrate in real time whether he or she has the abilities needed to do the work. Even where this kind of time is not available, an increasing number of companies are structuring interviews to simulate the challenges that the person will face.

A colleague of mine recently went through one of these sessions. She was asked to interpret the interviews and psychological tests of a hypothetical manager who was having difficulty at work, feed information from her interpretation back to that manager for his self-development, and then write up an evaluation of the whole procedure. The role of the manager was played by a vice president of the company where she was hoping to work, although his identity was unknown to my colleague.

The interviews and tests suggested that the manager had some difficulty with communication, although he brusquely dismissed that idea. My colleague was persistent, and he grew increasingly upset. Finally, he banged his hand down on the table and shouted, "All this talk about communication is just 'mouth-flapping!'" He followed that with several critical opinions about people who take "this HR, bleeding-heart, touchy-feely stuff" so seriously. She remained calm and offered the contrary view that his high-handed dismissal of "that stuff" had placed his career in jeopardy and that if he were serious about wanting to keep on working at his company, he'd do well to learn just a little more about it. He finished the interview in a more subdued manner . . . and she was hired.

Obviously, this company knew just what the role it was filling required: ability both to interpret tests and to coach a potentially angry manager. This company also knew how to discover whether a person had the abilities to fill that role. While you can't always know how a prospective employer plans to evaluate the necessary abilities, it is often possible to be clear in advance what abilities are being sought. That is part of the marketing-and-sales task that the dejobbed individual must learn to accomplish, and it's discussed in Chapters 7–9. Here my point is simply that dejobbing makes a prospective employer much more concerned about abilities and less concerned about education and experience than the old job-based employer was. The candidate needs to share that concern.

Instead of working on résumés based on the Three Es, candidates ought to do whatever is needed to gain a very clear picture of what abilities he or she brings to any potential client. The grandfather of career development, Bernard Haldane, called these abilities "dependable strengths," and the father of the field, Richard Bolles, called them "transferable skills." They are the structural element of both the work that an organization needs to get done and the work that your own D.A.T.A. equips you for.

Although there may indeed be technical skills—discussed under the heading of "Assets" in Chapter 6—that you need to acquire or to improve, you do not lack for abilities! In Chapter 2 I listed the ten abilities that recent research has identified as critical in today's workplace. They were things like reading and writing, remember? None of them involved gene splicing or software design. Only "computing" was a recent arrival, and my own experience with today's workers suggests that that ability is more widespread than effective writing is. So these abilities aren't esoteric.

That isn't to say that some of them aren't problematic. The number of young people who get through school without developing these basic abilities adequately makes it imperative for educational leaders to address this issue. But we must not let that need distract us from the plight of millions of workers who think they won't be able to find work because they don't have a master's in computer science or many years of experience on the World Wide Web. (Hey, stop being catastrophic! No one—yet—has many years of experience on the World Wide Web!)

SO . . . WHAT CAN YOU DO?

What can I do? That question causes most people either to start listing the things that their current job requires or else to go blank. I spent years stuck in those responses. In the early 1970s I wanted to leave my job as a college English teacher. What abilities did I have? "Teaching English at a college," I would have said, or (in another mood) "none." I couldn't get it through my head that there were abilities (Raul Fernandez called them "core talents") that I used every day, abilities without which teaching English would have been impossible.

It took me forever, it seemed, to learn that for as long as I could remember, my activities had been shaped by a cluster of basic abilities. They weren't fancy and visible like my school classmates' dancing talent or mathematical genius. My abilities were more general:

- I was pretty good at sensing people's motives.
- I could see the relations within a cluster of ideas.
- I was by nature pretty focused and hardworking.
- I was good at getting others to see things from new perspectives.
- I was a quick study, learning my way around a new subject fast.
- I was good at explaining things.

These abilities didn't show up on my résumé, but they were largely responsible for anything noteworthy that did.

I use my own case because I know it better than I know anyone else's. I also know how much time I lost by not understanding sooner what my real abilities were and how important it was for me to understand them. Having once learned what they were, I was able to make subsequent career moves much more quickly. But back then, I floundered around in the dark, making a little progress, and blazing my own trail without much help from guides or mentors. (Another ability of mine is doing everything myself. My wife could tell you that I often do that even when help is close at hand . . . and graciously offered.)

When one analyzes just how people move from one kind of work to another during their careers, one sees how abilities are recycled and reincarnated in one work situation after another. A recent *Wall Street Journal* article on career-changing lawyers made this point, quoting a Philadelphia career counselor named Douglas Richardson:

Anyone who has graduated from law school has very marketable skills employers are looking for. . . . You have strong oral and written communication skills, are adept at assessing needs and setting priorities, and you can think analytically.

The same article makes it clear that key abilities need not be the ones that the previous work utilized. "I still use my legal knowledge," says Robert

Saypol, a former attorney who is now a senior vice president with a mortgage banking firm, "but the talent that transferred best was salesmanship." Virginia Coombs, a civil litigation attorney who became the executive director of a community health care organization, drew on her "ability to negotiate and reach resolutions. . . . I can anticipate risk and minimize potential problems better than most" of her competitors for work.

Most people overlook such an article: "*I'm* not a lawyer. Do you have any articles on accountants? (or nursery school teachers or machinists or salespeople)?" they ask. They imagine that this is a content-based issue. It isn't. It is based on process, and the process you are using will work for chefs and heavy equipment drivers and assembly-line workers as well as for lawyers and doctors and architects. And it will work for you.

WHAT ARE *YOUR* ABILITIES?

Start as I did, with the work you are currently doing. It can be a regular job or occasional work for pay. It can also be volunteer work or the normal work around the home required to care for children and keep the household running. I'm using "work" in a very inclusive sense here to cover any activity that you do in order to achieve a practical result.

You can get inside such work and identify the abilities that go into it by asking several questions:

- What do you actually have to do to achieve your result?
- What "core talents" do you draw on to get the work done?
- When some particular aspect of that work goes well, what have you been doing to make it turn out that way?
- When people do well in this work arena, what do they have to be good at?

Imagine breaking down what you do in your work into the different abilities that make it up, the way you could reduce a compound to its constituent elements. That's the first question to answer: *What are the elemental abilities that enable you to do your work?*

But maybe the roles you play in the world of your work don't really let you use your abilities to the fullest. Maybe you use them in hobbies. (Collecting antiques, photography, square dancing, cooking, and wood carving all use different clusters of abilities.) Maybe you use them on committees at your church or as your child's soccer team coach or in home improvement projects. Write them down on pages 70–71.

SPOTTING YOUR ABILITIES IN ACTION

Method One

One of the signs of a fundamental ability is that when you are using it, it is easy for you to lose track of time. The feelings will vary with the circumstances: you may feel happy with what you are doing, you may feel as though you're working your tail off, or you may feel anxious about whether the results will be as good as you want them to be. Whatever you feel, you lose track of the time. Think of the last time you had that experience; then break down what you were doing into the ability or abilities that you were using then.

Method Two

Imagine that you are now that miniature company that we'll call You & Co. What are the "core competencies" of your company? What are the things that it does well, and what capacities does it take to do those things well? Since some of a company's core competencies involve working effectively with unusual or highly developed areas of knowledge, ask yourself what your company has in the way of a knowledge base. Restate it as an ability: "I am good at turning my knowledge of biochemistry (or poetry or real estate or mechanics or crowd psychology) into practical ways to do (whatever it is that you do)."

Method Three

Recall the years of your early childhood—up to the fourth grade or so. What abilities did you demonstrate when you were small? What were you good at?

- making peace between warring siblings
- getting your chores done quickly

- soothing yourself when you were upset
- picking up spelling rules quickly
- getting other kids to take part in your pastimes and fantasies
- talking your parents out of punishments
- organizing gang activities
- charming authority figures

Think about how you got through those years. It took a natural ability (at something) to do that.

There! What do you mean that you lack the abilities to do significant things?

My Abilities	Hobbies	Intellectual interests	Recreational activities
Abilities I regularly use in this activity			
Abilities that contribute to my particular enjoyment or success			
Abilities that people just seem to notice or appreciate			
Abilities that just come naturally to me			
Other abilities			

Family life	Friendships	Professional relationships	Schooling & professional development	Other significant activities

Your Temperament and Your Vocation

Rabbi Baer of Radoshitz once said to his teacher, the "Seer" of Lublin: "Show me one general way to the service of God."

The zaddik replied: "It is impossible to tell men what way they should take. For one way to serve God is through learning, another through prayer, another through fasting, and still another through eating. Everyone should carefully observe what way his heart draws him to, and then choose this way with all his strength."

—MARTIN BUBER, *THE WAY OF MAN*

TEMPERAMENT: THE CORE OF WHO YOU ARE

Throughout this book I have talked about the idea that each of us has a lifework, a kind of productive activity that is particularly fitting for us. Such work satisfies our unique desires, capitalizes on our singular abilities, and makes use of our individual assets. But the fit goes deeper than those things—it reaches down to how and what we are, to the structure and grain of our nature. I am choosing to call that aspect of ourselves our *temperament,* though I might have called it *personality, style,* or *character.* Whatever we call it, it is the very stuff that makes us *us.*

Temperament is what makes an individual prefer one kind of situation over another. Temperament is what makes one individual gravitate toward working with things, another gravitate toward working with information, and a third gravitate toward interpersonal work. Temperament is what gives an individual a characteristic style of approaching even very dif-

72

ferent learning situations—one choosing to amass a lot of information in advance and another to learn on the fly. Temperament is what gives an individual "identity"—which literally means "sameness," from one time to another and in all kinds of different contexts.

"There is," said the French writer, Jean Girardoux, "an invisible garment woven around us from our earliest years; it is made of the way we eat, the way we walk, the way we greet people." Ralph Waldo Emerson called this invisible garment our *character,* writing, "If you act, you show character; if you sit still, you show it; if you sleep, [you show it.]" Over two thousand years earlier, the Greek philosopher Heraclitus had used the same term: "A man's character," he wrote, "is his guardian divinity." Character—or, as we're calling it here, temperament—is the touchstone to which we must ever return.

This touchstone is indeed a kind of guardian, for it releases enormous energy when we are aligned with it and withholds most of our force when we are violating it. Your temperament is what makes a work situation feel "all wrong," even though it may utilize your abilities and assets effectively and even though it may seem to correspond with what you (only yesterday!) said that you desired.

This must have happened to you: You have been talking about wanting something, and then you get it and begin to act as though you don't want it. "I thought that this was what you wanted," says a puzzled friend.

"I know," you reply. "I do want it, but it just doesn't feel right."

ORGANIZATIONS TAKE TEMPERAMENT SERIOUSLY

The article on career-changing lawyers that I cited in the last chapter also alludes to the importance of temperament; it reports that career counselors find

> *lawyers are often too competitive with their colleagues to work well on a team, and so may not be best suited for general-management jobs. But . . . they do make great individual contributors for project-based and consulting assignments where they can call all the shots.*

In other words, the temperament that made a person successful in one job may prove to be a debit in another, but it also may be a boon in a project-based situation.

Because it is so difficult to define and because it can be used as a cover by others for discriminatory judgments, *temperament* is an easy concept to misuse. Think of the manager who rejects someone with these kinds of excuses:

- "She isn't the right kind of person for us."
- "He won't fit in here."
- "Her style isn't quite right."

All too often, such characterizations have meant (1) she's female, (2) he's black, or (3) she's older than the rest of the people in the office. Because temperament so easily becomes a stalking horse for discrimination, giving it weight feels dangerous and misleading to many people.

But temperament is a legitimate and a critical part of a person's qualifications, for it represents the way in which his or her *heart* can be engaged in and by work. There is no good word for what heart-engaged work does, although we could say that it *encourages* us and that work that doesn't engage our hearts *discourages* us; both those words come from *corage*, which is the Middle English word for "heart." *Desire* assures us that the will is engaged; *abilities* mean that the talents are engaged. But without a *temperamental* fit, something crucial is missing and the result cannot be satisfying for very long.

Many organizations recognize this fact. I have already given some crude and simple examples of how organizations factor in temperament: Nordstrom chooses the people who demonstrate "friendliness," for example, because it correlates with the customer service culture for which that retailer is famous. But it is not just in the soft-edged world of customer service that temperament counts. In the technically demanding world of Bell Labs, for example,

A study . . . found that the most valued and productive engineers working in teams weren't those with the highest IQ's or achievement test scores but those who excelled in rapport, empathy, cooperation, persuasion, and the ability to build consensus.

WHAT IS YOUR TEMPERAMENT?

Identifying your temperament is obviously an important question, and it is a hard one to answer. Type tests are useful: some people swear by the Myers Briggs Type Indicator (or MBTI), while others go for Enneagrams, and still others favor the conative-type system developed by Kathy Kolbe. Almost any test or indicator of that sort gives you a piece of the puzzle, and when you are assessing your D.A.T.A., you ought to use any of them that are available to you.

But becoming familiar with one's own temperament is not just a question of personality-type testing. Many other factors contribute to determining your temperament, and you can profit from thinking about all of them.

- You can learn a lot about your temperament by reading descriptions of the typical patterns exhibited by people who share your place in the family birth order. Firstborns share certain characteristics, as do middle children, youngest children, and only children.
- Your gender contributes significantly to your temperament. Few people can read books such as Deborah Tannen's *You Just Don't Understand* or John Gray's *Men Are from Mars, Women Are from Venus* without seeing some of their characteristics spelled out clearly.
- Temperament is also affected by ethnic or cultural heritage, so much so that people talk about the French, the Japanese, or the English temperament. Although these generalizations are often much too broad to be trusted in detail, they undeniably reflect actual and widely shared differences between people from different backgrounds.
- Historical factors also shape temperament. We talk about the Depression mentality, meaning that people brought up in the United States during the 1930s were marked by the anxieties and uncertainties of that decade. Today's "twentysomethings" (or Generation X) likewise share a common set of influences, as does the generation that came of age during the Eisenhower years or during the Vietnam War. Chapter 1 noted how the temperamental factors shared by many baby boomers have helped to create the dejobbed workplaces that many of us are trying to adjust to.

■ Don't overlook your friends' everyday reactions as a source of insight into your temperament. You get feedback on your temperament every time one of them asks, "Why did you think that?" or "How come you always want to do that?"

The question of temperament is not something that a chapter on the subject can answer. My purpose here is simply to argue that you need to become more sensitive to your own temperament and how it affects the way in which you are *encouraged* or *discouraged* by different kinds of work. My purpose is not so much to urge you to discover some objective answer ("You are meant to be a doctor") as it is to argue that your temperamentally based reactions are a constant source of information on whether you are on or off course in your lifework journey.

STAYING CLEAR OF BURNOUT

In 1981, an influential industrial psychologist named Dr. Harry Levinson wrote an article for the *Harvard Business Review* called "When Executives Burn Out." The phenomenon of "burnout" was not so widely discussed back then as (in part because of this article) it has been since. The article became one of what the magazine calls its "classics," articles of which readers frequently request reprints. So, as they do with these classics, the *HBR* editors reprinted the article many years after it was written, with an afterword in which Levinson observed how the situation had changed in the fifteen intervening years.

It had changed so much, he wrote, that the whole premise of the article was invalid today. Organizations no longer looked out for their employees, so employees had to look out for themselves. Burnout was an even bigger problem today than it had been then, but today it was up to the individual to develop a plan for avoiding it. That plan, Levinson wrote, will have to forgo any reliance on job related technical skills: "A specific skill will never be an enduring source of self-reliance, because it risks losing its value in the marketplace."

Instead, individuals must build their work lives around what he calls "characteristic behaviors," which are (as one can see when he illustrates them with a list) just the kinds of characteristics that we have been calling temperamental:

Whether we are naturally levelheaded, spontaneously enthusiastic, artlessly charming, or born to persevere, we take our behaviors with us into everything we do. If what you do is at the core of who you are, your stress level will go down.

Whether you call it *character* or *characteristic behaviors* or *temperament,* it is clear that whatever you are personally must be factored into what you are professionally.

In the past, organizations frowned on employees who did that. Today— due to the holdover of old attitudes—organizations don't always reward temperament-based work choices. But the best work that is being done today is being done by people who are working with (and not across) the grain of their temperament. And an increasing number of companies are taking that fact seriously enough to encourage it in their hiring practices.

Whether or not a prospective employer has understood the imperative to align tasks with people's predispositions, you will simply be unable to compete in today's workplace unless you have done that. It's the modern version of the ancient imperative to "know thyself" and the admonition, "To thine own self be true." Socrates and Shakespeare, the respective authors of the two phrases, certainly didn't have the world of the modern corporation in mind when they said what they said. But that may not be accidental, because the "modern" corporation was job-based. In this post-job world, it may be ancient wisdom that is the most reliable.

WHAT DOES YOUR TEMPERAMENT TELL YOU?

In fact, temperament seldom leads you to the specific field you would be happy working in. Forget the dream that you are by nature intended to be a doctor or an entrepreneur or a retail worker. Think, instead, that temperament tells you which approach you'll be happiest taking within the field that you chose for other reasons.

Although your temperament won't tell you if you'd be successful and happy as a physician, it can help you to choose whether *as a physician* you'd thrive most as a researcher, an administrator, a psychotherapist, a pathologist, an orthopedic surgeon, or a family doctor. Your temperament won't help you to decide whether a department store is the right place for you to work, but it may help you to figure out whether you'd be more satisfied working as a salesperson, a bookkeeper, a floor supervisor, a buyer, a tailor, a customer service specialist, or the person who creates the window displays.

Forget the idea that learning about your temperament will settle the question of whether or not you have it in you to be an entrepreneur. But consider the possibility that such knowledge may help you focus in on the right approach for you to take to your entrepreneurial venture. Here are the reasons different people, with different temperaments, might set out to be entrepreneurs:

- to capitalize on a wide network of business contacts
- to create the financial resources for a new venture
- to sell the world on something that they believe in
- to create, invent, or imagine solutions to customers' problems
- to run an undertaking without interference from the jerks who insist on explaining "how we do it at ABC Industries"

A QUESTION TO ASK YOURSELF

Temperament is a jewel with many facets. No test or sorting principle can do much more than give you the view of the subject through one of those facets. Needless to say, any particular view obscures some things at the same time that it highlights other things. But that is OK. This exploration of your temperament is an ongoing process (remember?), not a procedure designed to give you a fixed answer.

Whether you are taking a test, listening to feedback from a friend, or just thinking about your temperament, you are really trying to answer one basic question: "What kind of a person am I?" This is different from figuring out your identity, "Who am I?", by listing the key roles, relationships, and affiliations in your life. Forget Presbyterian, Democrat, southerner, and state university graduate. I'm talking about *what kind of person you are*.

- Are you someone who likes to figure things out for yourself, or is the give and take of a collegial group a big part of work for you?

- Do you like to break new ground and try the untried, or do you like to perform or produce according to some tried or tested way?
- Would you rather focus your work on situations that keep the human factor to a minimum, or is it precisely the "human factor" that you like to deal with?
- Do you carry out activities mainly to reach whatever outcome you are seeking, or do you carry out the activities primarily for the pleasure they inherently give you?

There are a hundred other question clusters you could use to guide you in exploring *what kind of person you are.* Take the following suggestions as examples, therefore, and not necessarily as the path to follow. Ask your own questions about yourself, or do so if they are helpful and don't if they aren't. Either way, spend some time thinking about *what kind of person you are.*

Step One

Jot down your thoughts in answer to the question, *"What Kind of Person Am I?"* Don't worry about coherence or logic. And don't try to edit your list as you go. Let the phrases, words, and sentences stand just as they came from your head. Use the shortest phrases you can to capture your idea—single words are fine if they make sense to you. Pretend you're writing newspaper headlines.

Build one idea on another. You say that you are "well organized"? Does a thought flit past that you're just a tiny bit "compulsive" too? And "obsessive"—even though it was only in that nasty argument with your sister that that word was used? Write *everything* down. Let a stream-of-consciousness quality develop in this activity, so that you write whatever you think and use whatever you write as a springboard to more thinking.

Keep going for as long as you can without artificially forcing the process. If you aren't in the mood, set the paper aside and come back to it later. If you hate the exercise, write, "I am a person who hates exercises like this!" But then use that as a springboard. Why do you hate them? What do you prefer? (You say that you're the kind who hates all of this *introspection* and *self-analysis?* Fine. Write that down. And then follow it with what kinds of things a person like you prefers.) You get the idea.

Step Two

Put this paper away. But don't lose it. (If you do, get a new piece of paper and start with, "I am the kind of person who loses whatever I don't like to think about," and build on that!)

After a few days, take out that paper and read it over. Who is this bozo who wrote those words, *"What Kind of Person?"* If the paper had been written by somebody else, what would you say about his or her temperament? Be a detective.

You may feel that, as far as temperament is concerned, this person isn't playing with a full deck. You may be tempted to give up on this character (suggested career: unemployment). But use your imagination a little. Good careers aren't the result of being dealt terrific cards—only of playing well whatever cards you are dealt.

Step Three

Write down the three or four things that stand out for you as temperamentally important for the work life of this person who wrote the list. Don't try to get ideas about the work itself, just the qualities of the work or the situation that would fit or "go with the grain" of this person. And remember: there is no such a thing as a person without a temperament or one who is temperamentally disabled. Every negative characteristic has its flipside. The "disorganized" person may have a quirky, creative side. The person who "can't settle down" may thrive in a work life where projects follow one another quickly, and the person who "doesn't want to change" may do very well in a situation where a project is replicated over and over again in different parts of an organization.

So . . . what's the temperament card in your own hand?

CHAPTER SIX

Identifying Your Assets

as·set: 1. A useful or valuable quality or thing. 2. A valuable item that is owned.

—AMERICAN HERITAGE DICTIONARY OF THE ENGLISH LANGUAGE

WHAT ARE "ASSETS"?

One of the advantages of the D.A.T.A. system of career development is that it redefines qualification in a way that shows people that they are, in fact, "well qualified" for work that needs doing today. This is true, furthermore, without any of the mind-manipulating techniques through which some other approaches seek to convince people that they can "think," "affirm," or "believe" their way to success—in spite of lacking the usual qualifications for getting ahead in a world like ours.

The D.A.T.A. system begins with something we all undeniably have: Desires. It goes on to emphasize the Abilities everyone has been using since childhood and the Temperament that everyone has just by nature. But then we get to Assets. There, you may feel, we hit the snag—because you don't have any Assets, beyond what's left of your paycheck and a car that is slowly expiring. Oh, maybe the ring that your mother gave you for graduation. Assets? Very few.

That view is all wrong. It defines *asset* in the traditional, narrow, economic sense—meaning number two in the dictionary entry quoted above. That meaning of *asset* used to fit the world of jobs well enough, but it is no longer useful. We're no longer accumulating the wherewithal to buy something; we're assembling the resources from which to create something. The "assets" we are interested in will never show up on a loan application. They are aspects of you, your situation, or your life history that you could use to your advantage in today's workplace.

These things are unlike traditional assets, in that their value is dependent upon the situation. A house with $45,000 equity in it is an asset, worth that much regardless of what you want to do with the money. But aspects of your life history may be worth nothing in one situation and everything in another situation.

A decade ago, Amy Quirk was a hospital administrator and Eric Weiss was a medical resident. If you had asked them their vocationally relevant assets, they would have had plenty to talk about, but their experience and passion for "extreme kayaking," that is, whitewater paddling in dangerous situations, would not have been on the list. After all, they were medical people, not professional outdoors people. But their hobby was an asset that gave them a knowledge of a niche that needed a product, and their education gave them the expertise to fill it. So they started producing emergency medical kits for adventure travelers and sports enthusiasts. Their product line now extends through sixty kit types, from a $6 econo-model to a $400 version for paramedics.

Imagine, for example, that you are looking for work at two different companies. One is a traditional company that still hired on the Three E system. You fill out the application and are then interviewed by someone in Personnel. The person wants to know just what kind of companies you have worked for: were they "good," "successful" companies? Just what jobs did you hold, and how long did you spend in each of them? Who were your supervisors and what are their phone numbers? And, incidentally, how many years of schooling have you had, and what subject was your Ph.D. in?

Now imagine that the other company is Microsoft. You go in for your "interview" and find that it's actually half a dozen conversations with people at various levels—real workers, not Personnoids. The last one is a guy in a sports shirt, and you're actually sitting down when you realize he just introduced himself as "Bill Gates!" Yes, like a lot of people leading de-jobbed organizations, the CEO of Microsoft likes to participate in the hiring process. He asks all kinds of questions.

"What excites you?" You're not quite sure how to answer that one, although a couple of obviously inappropriate answers cross your mind. Then, "How much water flows though the Mississippi River each day?" You're sweating now. And finally, "Did you ever work for a company that was going down the tubes, going out of business, failing?" What is he getting at? Is he asking if you're a loser? Should you say no, or should you talk about that time seven years ago when you spent a year at a computer renting firm that went bankrupt?

With the first two questions, the answer hardly matters. It is what you show as you answer the question. *What excites you?* You can reveal a good deal about what you Desire and what your Temperament is. *How much water?* You are being asked to demonstrate your Ability to think your way toward a response to a question that no one would know the answer to. And the third question is about an Asset.

What asset? Your experience working for a failing company at some time during your career. Here is Gates himself talking about that asset:

> *Being in a successful company is easy. But when you're failing you're forced to be creative, and to dig deep and think. In failing companies you always have to question assumptions. I want some people around who have been through that process.*

Now, you might always have considered that little segment of your career to be one of your debits, but here it suddenly turns up on the asset side of your ledger.

The asset may even be something that you don't accept as important or even valid—but if your customer does, you need to accept it as a resource. Virginia Coombs, a civil litigation lawyer quoted in Chapter 4, discovered this twice. The first time was when she was asked why she was leaving the law. Realizing that it makes a potential customer nervous if you denigrate your last work situation, she answered, "I didn't criticize the law. Instead, I said I had a responsibility to my youngest child to find a less demanding schedule, and people were so admiring of my sacrifice, they never questioned my reasoning." She also found that she had an asset that she had never thought of because of her law degree: "Interviewers think I'm smarter than if I was a teacher or nurse, which isn't fair, but that's what they think."

So I really meant it when I defined an asset as "any aspect of you, your situation, or your life history that you could use to your advantage in today's workplace." And that is why I said that there was no way to give you a list of possible assets from which to check off your own. The list would be longer than this book. It would have to be updated daily with the discoveries that are being made by all the people who are repositioning themselves to seize the opportunities being created by the great jobshift that is taking place today.

YOU HAVE A ZILLION ASSETS

Every piece of knowledge you have is an asset—as is knowing any field of knowledge fairly well. You won't get to use it on a quiz, and you may not even get to show it off. But knowing something, understanding how something works, recognizing a pattern of ideas because you have encountered them before—these would all be assets *in the right situation*. (Keep in mind the situational nature of assets. They aren't what credit cards claim to be . . . accepted everywhere!)

Skills

Your specialized skills are assets. A skill in working with C++ computer language could be an asset at Microsoft. In a research setting in which my daughter worked, a skill with a bar coder—a handheld variant of the electronic gizmos they use in grocery checkout lines—was such an essential skill that people had to forget doing any research until they acquired it.

"Wait a minute," you say. "You told me to forget about those sorts of skills back when we were talking about abilities, and concentrate instead on more basic things that I've been able to do since I was a kid." Right. The abilities that'll get you hired are the things that make you productive, the things that enable you to solve problems, the things that make a team function better just because you're on it. But organizations look for assets too, and technical skills are—in the right situation—definite assets.

Now start to tally up your potential assets. Let's say you learned Tagalog in preparation for your Peace Corps assignment. Asset! (Though that is true only, of course, in situations where the ability to speak with Filipinos is useful.)

How about the simple bookkeeping you learned during your summer job as an office helper? (It may turn out that none of the other people being considered by the founder of the tiny biotechnical start-up can even keep a checkbook in balance!)

And the piloting skill that you picked up during your ill-starred high school dream of becoming an airline pilot? What if you were proposing yourself as an assistant to a CEO who liked to pilot his own plane? ("Hmm . . . you know how to fly? That's very interesting!")

Don't imagine that these skills have to be rare or complex. I suppose that the two skills that I've used most often professionally have been two that I didn't want to acquire and certainly didn't enjoy acquiring: typing and public speaking. I am typing or rather, because I use a computer, key-boarding, right now. I've used this skill almost every day since I started earning a living. At first I used it as a teacher and then, when I went into business for myself, I kept on using it because I couldn't afford to pay any-one to do it for me. Now I can't write unless I keyboard. Since this is my ninth book, I'd have to say that having learned to type made my dejobbed work life possible.

My whole professional life as a consultant and trainer also depends on the things I learned in that dumb high school public speaking course. I didn't want to take it. I endured depressions before assigned speeches and anxiety attacks whenever I stood in front of the class while it debated what topic to give me for an extemporaneous speech. You know, the ones that begin when the teacher says, "THREE . . . TWO . . . ONE . . . Mr. Bridges is going to talk to us today about . . . WOOD BY-PRODUCTS!" But now I give about fifty speeches a year.

DEGREES AND CREDENTIALS

In Chapter 2 I said that the Three Es were useless today, but I was exaggerating a little. That graduate degree you got won't be wasted, especially if it qualifies you for a credential. In fact, the credential may be the asset without which you wouldn't be in the running for whatever work you are going after. But even when that is so, you are going to have to turn it into a product for some market.

I'll get to the product in Part III. The point I want to make here is that you shouldn't automatically decide that you will need to go back to school to prepare yourself for a place in the dejobbed world. There are a lot of folks out there doing remarkably well with nothing more than the education or training that you already have. And there are a lot of folks doing miserably with a good deal more education than you'll probably ever have—folks who don't understand what's happening, folks who keep mumbling, "Here I am with a master's degree in economics (or Spanish, or forestry), and I have to drive a cab to put food on the table!"

What such people don't understand is that the changes that we are calling "dejobbing" mean that education no longer provides you with an *automatic* advantage. Its benefits are now *provisional*. That is, the benefits depend on the existence of a goal or purpose to which the education in question is directly relevant. This is a huge shift and not, as it happens, an altogether positive one. When we treated education as simply one part of the growing-up and coming-of-age process, we each learned many things that only later turned out to be relevant. If the purpose of education changes, will we still have the backlog of knowledge to do something we didn't dream of back then?

A personal example: when I went to school, Latin was a standard part of the college preparatory curriculum. Although I couldn't conceive of any purpose for taking four years of Latin back then, it has made a difference in my career since. Studying Latin taught me how language develops over time. When I discussed the meaning of *encourage* in Chapter 5, I was drawing on that education. I drew on that education when, in *JobShift*, I traced the strange development of the word *job:* (1) a Celtic word for mouth or "gob" of something in the mouth; (2) then applied to a hunk, a bunch, or a pile of anything; (3) then transferred to whatever one did with that pile of stuff; (4) finally, to any kind of task or undertaking. That's where things stood at the dawn of the factory age. A *job-man* was someone you hired to do a particular task—a contractor or a temp, in modern terms. Only after 1800 came the meaning we give to *job* today.

There were a lot of very positive things about the world in which there were "jobs" that you expected your education to "prepare you for." Today many of the people who did well in that world are sad, confused, and more than a little bitter about its disappearance. But there were also some nasty things about that world, and one of them was that if your family resources or values didn't permit you to get an education when you were young, you were at a real disadvantage. If this was your own case, then you may well find that the dejobbed world is, comparatively speaking, a world full of opportunity for you. We are all—Ph.D.'s and high school dropouts alike—going to be putting together what we have to offer from our D.A.T.A., and education per se is no longer a ticket to the party.

Education still confers benefits: it may provide you with your own equivalent of my typing, public speaking, and Latin; it may introduce you to your future spouse or the person who invites you in on the ground floor of a new business venture; it may even train you in a field that you parlay into a career. And we mustn't overlook its public relations value. I could do all that I currently do professionally without my three degrees from Ivy League institutions. But I would be kidding myself if I pretended that I could have had the same credibility in my field without them. I have to admit that I list them on my résumé, but I often feel like an impostor, since that education didn't prepare me for my present career.

Education is an asset, but so are a lot of other things. You've probably read the old argument that a college education is worth the money because people with college degrees make so much more during their lifetimes than people without them do: about $600,000, in fact. Well, that's true, and six hundred grand isn't peanuts. But it's also true that if you took the money that getting that degree costs and invested it in mutual funds, you'd end up with much more money at the end of your career.

I'm not urging you to forget college. For one thing, it's hard to get the basic skills you'll need anywhere else. For another, higher education can open your eyes to possibilities that you'd otherwise miss. And although this may rank low on your current to-do list, it can make you a much more *interesting* person to both others and yourself. And that quality is a real asset.

I am simply saying that as an asset, education is useful only when it is useful. Similarly, the equity in your house is useful if you want to borrow money to start a business or to support your family for a while, but not very useful if you're trying to talk your way into a company as the solution to its current problem with customer complaints. To assess anything's asset value, you need to have at least a general idea of what you are trying to do in your market with the D.A.T.A. that you've been dealt.

EXPERIENCES

Occasionally, of course, there are assets that are just too rare not to be starting points for your planning: like being seven feet two and very coordinated; like having native fluency in the language of an important emerging nation; like owning a process for desalinating seawater quickly and cheaply. Lacking those kinds of assets myself, I had to look elsewhere when I was getting ready to leave teaching. I assume you will too.

As I started my own You & Co. (before I had ever imagined that concept), I was obsessed by the fact that except for summer jobs and two years as a supply-room clerk in the army, I'd had no nonteaching experience. It was a vicious circle. I wanted to leave teaching, and my résumé made it clear that I was a well-qualified teacher. In job terms, that is. I had other experiences that were gold, though it took me almost a decade to learn how to mine them.

I had set up and run a two-week summer seminar for college teachers who, like me, were fed up with the traditional teaching they had been trained to do. As we'll see in Chapter 7, the market that many people do best in is that of people with the same kind of problems that they have. Most of my fellow English professors tried to talk me out of the project, but once I got past the unfamiliarity of talking several groups into sponsoring my conference (public speaking helped), assembling a big mailing list (which I typed myself), inviting speakers I didn't know (famous psychologist Abraham Maslow accepted!), I found that I wasn't too bad at conference creating.

When I left teaching, I did two things that proved very useful. First, I began to glimpse the rudiments of D.A.T.A. analysis and to start identifying what resources I had that I could really rely on. Second, I kept thinking of the experience of creating my summer conference. At first, I drew on it for modest seminars entitled "How to Deal Successfully with Personal Transition." Then I branched out to offer the seminar to workers at a government agency that was in the midst of a big change. Then I thought of putting on a big public conference on a subject that was interesting me more and more, which was how different times during the life cycle seemed to be times of transition. Gail Sheehy's book *Passages* had made the subject a somewhat popular one, and I thought I might find a hundred people or so who'd pay to spend a weekend hearing talks about it.

Once again, friends and coworkers tried to talk me out of the project. It was a long shot. I'd be risking my own money. Only big sponsors like a university could pull this kind of thing off. But:

- I really, really wanted to do it. The Desire was clear.
- I ran through the Abilities: the ability to get people I didn't know to collaborate in something I really believed in had brought Maslow on board my first conference. This time it brought aboard half a dozen specialists, including Carl Rogers and Elizabeth Kubler-Ross.
- This kind of event drew on some element of my Temperament that likes to create things, prefers to work outside the organizational boundaries, and can hardly resist doing what people say won't work.
- I had an Asset in my experience with conference creating. The mailing list was much bigger this time, but it was the same process. Publicizing the conference with press interviews and talks before interested groups—that was just typing and public speaking all over again.

The results of my second conference were different. This time the attendance wasn't the 33 participants I'd been so happy with the first time, or even the 100 attendees I had aimed for. This time 1,700 people came!

I use this example because I know it so well and to assure you that I have practiced what I preach. Like any example, however, it runs the risk of seeming like something that you ought to copy. Don't. It's the *process* that you ought to copy. Forget the results . . . except when you get a little discouraged after people tell you that your idea won't work. Forget the results, because they are specific to one particular person's D.A.T.A. I've been talking here about assets that are not the same as yours. But you have experiences, so you have assets.

Any experience can be an Asset if it is harnessed to Desire, if it is supported by your Abilities, and if it fits your Temperament. Having experienced the horrors of fighting in Vietnam became Assets for people who Desired to create support services for veterans who had been deeply scarred by the same experience. Experience fighting an addiction is an Asset for anyone who wants to help other addicts. They are no less (and no more) valuable than the Asset of being an Olympic gold medalist or knowing an assistant adviser at the White House. Anything can be an Asset:

- anything you have ever done before
- anyone you know, even slightly, even at second hand
- any place that you have ever been
- anything you know, regardless of how you learned it

That you grew up with a retarded sister can be, in the right situation, an Asset. That you had a painful, lonely childhood can be an Asset. That you spent your junior year of high school in Mexico. That you once long-jumped twenty-four feet. That you ran a successful bake sale at your church. That animals like you. That you could qualify for a minority-owned business loan. That you had two years of Portuguese in college. That you look older (or younger) than you are.

Even your personality defects can be assets—in the right situation. As the French writer Alexis de Tocqueville wrote, "We succeed in enterprises which demand the positive qualities we possess, but we excel in those which can also make use of our defects." Even our neuroses can serve us well in the right circumstance. You may be ashamed of your obsessiveness, but if someone needs absolute reliability and utter regularity, you're just what the doctor ordered. Paranoia is going to be a debit in most situations, but what about someone who's trying to build a security system? Your codependence may drive your family crazy, but there are countless executives who will pay good money for the kind of preoccupation with someone else's welfare that is the hallmark of codependency.

You get the point. Now you need to identify your own Assets.

ASSAYING YOUR ASSETS

You are going to have to revisit the question of assets periodically during your career review. Since they are only true "assets" in the context of a particular situation, you will have to postpone your ultimate identification of your Assets until after you see the unmet needs of your chosen market. But it won't do simply to forget the question of assets completely until then. You need to have at least a general idea of your D.A.T.A. when you begin to evaluate your potential markets. It's a chicken-and-egg situation:

your assets contribute to your product, which can be created only after your market review; but your assets may suggest markets that you ought to explore and may even suggest products that you ought to try to develop.

Here are some suggestions for a first-pass review of your assets. Return to this task after you have done your market review. By then you'll have more of an idea of what's needed out there, so you can be both more selective in inventorying your assets (i.e., some won't be very relevant to the markets you are considering) and much more intensive in your consideration of the assets that could potentially contribute to your product.

Step One

What is unusual about you? Not *weird,* but a little out of the ordinary, involving something that not everybody is or has or does. It might be your size. It might be the skydiving or reading Russian novels or wood carving that you do. It might be the fact that you can draw recognizable likenesses of people or high-jump over six feet or cast a dry fly a long way. It might be that you are short and wiry and agile, or that you are huge and powerful. It might be that you are a military veteran or a Native American or a vegetarian. It might be that you are a whiz at computer games, or that you can sing like an angel, or that you're an exceptionally good cook. It might be any characteristic or accomplishment or capacity that is a little distinctive. Without trying to decide what possible help these could be to you now, jot them down.

Step Two

The first list covers you in the present. Now think of yourself in the past. There are things that you have accomplished, people you have known, places you have been. There are the experiences you have had. All of these might, in the right context, represent assets. This is tricky since you have no context yet. You really ought to write out every conceivable asset, but that would take forever, so use the following form to organize your thoughts:

	Personal experiences	Work experiences	Achievements	Projects
Years 0–5				
6–10				
11–15				
16–20				
20s				
30s				
40s				
50s				
60s				
70s				
80s				

Go through your life chronologically, down the vertical time blocks in the first column of this table, and jot down words or phrases under each of the headings, capturing quickly the time line of each of the four categories:

1. *Personal experiences*—travel, changes in living arrangements, relationships, illnesses, new interests or activities, reversals of fortune, spiritual turnings, or "time outs."

2. *Work experiences*—both formal and informal, both jobs and volunteer activities, both paid and domestic, i.e., anything "productive."

3. *Achievements*—both consciously undertaken (climbing a mountain, getting a sought-after job, making a sports team, getting an essay published) and less formally undertaken (making the honor roll, getting over your asthma, coming out of a depression, being named employee of the month).

4. *Projects*—work-related and personal, assigned and self-initiated, big and small, rewarded and unnoticed—anything with a beginning, middle and an end, where the activity and not the result is the notable thing. Things notable for their results belong under *achievements*.

Step Three

Set the sheet aside for a day so that you can return to it with a fresh eye. Then go through it slowly. Savor and consider the entry you've made in each square. Each of those entries is an asset in the rough. You have to "husk it," remove the incidental and the superficial content, and find the asset within. For instance, what if you spent a semester in business school but dropped out? That abbreviated experience may in fact have given you more formal management knowledge than most people in your field. What if you spent every weekend for several months working for a political referendum campaign? Regardless of whether it was successful or not, that project could have left you with skills, experience, or contacts that can be assets.

In some cases the asset won't be much, but in other cases it will be very significant. Your task is to convert the situation and the events to a learning experience that you could apply to other circumstances and different contexts. This is going to take some time. It's less like a formal procedure and more like a guided reflection. Keep a list of your findings, cross-indexed to the chronological chart, for further reflection later.

Step Four

Go back through the chronological table and ask yourself if it doesn't contain information about the rest of your D.A.T.A.

- What Desires show up on the list that you still have? Maybe you had forgotten them. Maybe they got lost in life's busyness. Maybe you didn't even understand, back then, what it was you really desired.
- What Abilities enabled you to do those things? Pick them apart, look for the activities that went into them, then melt the activities down into the Abilities you used to reach the outcomes.
- What does this verbal roadmap of your life say about your Temperament? What kind of a bird were you back when you were younger? In what sense is that younger person still around? What's the nature, the style, the "grain," the temperament of that younger person?

Any discoveries you make here should be carried back to the appropriate place in the book and added to what you learned about your Desires, Abilities, and Temperament back then.

Step Five

Here's a list of hypothetical clients that You & Co. might be able to serve, if only you could identify which one of your Assets they each needed. Use these examples to stimulate your thinking about what in your past could be made into an asset for your future.

A. Broot Beer, the maker of a ferociously sweet, award-winning root beer, wants to expand its market. The company is locked out of the major restaurant chains, which already have root beer suppliers.

B. Terry L. Jefferson is running for Congress. A bright, articulate, and committed activist whose positions you agree with, Johnson is nonetheless viewed by the public as a less than serious candidate.

C. Your neighbor shares some disturbing news: because of budget cutbacks in the capital, in three months the public afterschool day-care program won't have enough money to pay all of its staff.

Step Six

Go through the preceding exercises with a spouse, other relative, or close friend. Ideally, this partner should be someone who has known you for a long time or is familiar with your past. Explain the idea of assets, and ask this person to help you identify yours. Or each of you could help the other to identify assets that he or she has. Often, we don't recognize our own resources as easily as other people do.

PART THREE

TURNING YOUR D.A.T.A.
INTO A PRODUCT

Find the biggest problem your employer faces for which you and your skills are the solution.

—ROBERT HORTON, EXECUTIVE RECRUITER

This part of the book will help you develop products for You & Co. But before you start thinking about products, you need to determine the unmet needs you are going to address. That will be the topic of Chapter 7, "Finding Your Opportunity." When you've decided who your clients are going to be and what their needs actually are, then we can talk about the product you're selling and the business you are actually in.

Spelling it out in this sequence is the only way to learn how to do it, but in fact it's more like a circle where you can begin anywhere and where everything leads on to everything else. Your D.A.T.A. is meaningless without a situation to use it in, and the situation is irrelevant if you don't have appropriate D.A.T.A. to respond to it. Maybe when we get all this material on hypertext, you'll be able to start anywhere and go through the elements in any order. But this is a book, so we're stuck with a linear format for now.

Finding Your Opportunity

Marketing is an attitude, not a department.
—PHIL WEXLER

WHAT IS YOUR MARKET?

As I've worked with people whose jobs are threatened by the changes we discussed in Chapter 1, I've sometimes asked them what their markets were. Almost without exception, they've replied in terms of the markets served by the organizations where they had a job—"automobile buyers," "individual investors with incomes over $75,000," or "parents with young children." Most of the people added that they didn't know a lot about all that stuff because they weren't "in marketing."

When I have said that I wasn't referring to their company's markets but *theirs,* most of them have looked puzzled. The more sophisticated ones have started talking about how people at their company were being urged to be more market-focused these days, so they guessed that their activities had to have some impact on the company's presence in the market. Their employer's market was, in that sense, *their* market. Was that what I meant? I seldom had the heart to say no again, so we'd lapse into chit-chat about how market-driven organizations were these days, even schools and churches!

What I was trying to get at was something quite different. Because of the changes discussed in Chapter 1, companies are no longer viewing their employees as automatically the best people to do the work that needs

101

doing. Almost any work that now accounts for the "jobs" within a company can be outsourced. If the work in question is brief in duration, the company can hire temps, contractors, or consultants to do it.

Those external people don't have "jobs." They are freelancers who see the world inside the organization as a market. They operate like little one-person businesses and the organization *is* their market. They look at the world within the organization with what Theodore Levitt called "the marketing imagination." The more successful they are in their roles, the more they see the office or the factory floor as a market made up of people looking for ways to get their needs met.

When I said earlier that in the postjob world employees need to forget their jobs and start looking for the work that needs doing, I was saying that they must develop this same marketing imagination. If they don't, they are likely to lose their work to someone who isn't a conventional employee but has the marketer's point of view toward the work that needs doing.

Because this represents a big shift in outlook for most workers, and because the marketing element in dejobbed careers is so important, let me spell these ideas out in a dozen straightforward statements:

1. "Marketing" (as I am using the term here) doesn't refer to the organization's market; it refers to the dejobbed individual's market. Your task as a dejobbed worker is to discover what market your D.A.T.A. best prepares you to serve.

2. Your market isn't "the job market," nor is it necessarily your organization's customers. Your market is, rather, the people around you who have unmet needs. Identifying those unmet needs is your main task as a marketer.

3. You need to view the rapidly changing world around you as a pattern of overlapping markets, imagining as you do so that you are a small business looking for a niche. You aren't looking for "jobs," but rather "opportunities." Opportunities are simply unmet needs that your own D.A.T.A. would enable you to meet or fill or satisfy.

4. This means that even when you are employed, you should stop thinking like an employee and start thinking like an opportunity-minded vendor. An "employee" does his or her job, working on

"special" projects if asked to but returning to the job for security and identity. In contrast, a "vendor," being in business for him- or herself, is constantly scanning the market for the work that needs doing. The security and identity that we all need come from the little one-person business that a vendor develops.

5. Since organizations are unbundling their activities more and more, every employee is in direct (though often unacknowledged) competition with external vendors who would be happy to bring the vendor's mindset to any task currently being done by an employee.

6. To actual vendors, boundaries are mere formalities: inside and outside, this department and that mean little. It's all a market full of people with unmet needs and (on the other side of the transaction) full of resource providers who could be collaborators or coventurers in the task the vendor is undertaking.

7. To compete with these vendors, you need to forget your job and look at your fellow employees in and out of your department as customers with unmet needs and as coventurers. You need to shift your focus from your job to a product that meets your client's needs. (I'll talk about how to do that in the next chapter.)

8. Once you start seeing your organization as a collection of many overlapping markets, you see that markets are all around you in every part of your life. Your profession is a market. People like you are a market. Your former organization is a market. Your present job world is only one of your potential markets, because you are surrounded by many others.

9. Obviously, marketing involves communication, but don't start with what you want to communicate to your market. Start with what the market is trying to tell *you*. Think of markets as fields of messages waiting to be decoded—with success going to the decoder who can translate the underlying message (combined with his or her D.A.T.A.) into a useful product.

10. You need to understand that while change is the enemy of people who are trying to hold on to their jobs, it is the friend of people who take this marketing approach. Change constantly creates new unmet needs. It destroys opportunities only for the "employee-

minded" person; for the "vendor-minded," it simply *relocates* opportunity.

11. This process of relocating opportunity goes on constantly in the big, public market of a free enterprise economy. Old companies are constantly dying and new ones are being born because an old opportunity area has closed up here and a new one has opened up over there. "Dejobbing" is simply the same process occurring within an organization.

12. This means that career planning needs to be a process very similar to the strategic business planning within a small start-up company that is trying to capitalize on changes in its market: You & Co. For an actual strategic planning process for your own little company, see Chapter 9.

Could *You* Do This?

As you read the twelve statements above, you may acknowledge that they make sense logically, but you may be doubting that you (or "ordinary workers" in general) could change your whole approach to work so completely. I'll answer your doubts in three ways. First, I have to acknowledge that the shift I'm talking about *is* a huge one and that you have to go back to the advent of jobs at the start of the Industrial Revolution to find one that is as large. You'll find some suggestions to make that shift easier in Chapter 10, "Making Your Plan and Getting Started."

Second, I want to remind you that the people who filled those early jobs were quite unready for their new experience too. They had never worked regular hours before. They had never done the same thing over and over again, as the so-called division of labor requires most job holders to do. They had never experienced the vulnerability of being totally dependent on wages, which could be canceled at any time. It was not that the new world of jobs was harder or worse than the life of the small farmer or craftsperson—though people then often argued that it was—but simply that it was very different and that the transition from the old way of working to the new way was wrenching. So it is today. To be born at one of history's infrequent turning points is a daunting experience.

Third, I'd like you to consider some of the people who have already made that shift, so that you can see that they aren't unusually gifted or free-spirited. For example, let me tell you about an elderly African-American man who works at the airport in Atlanta. He doesn't have a job there, although in 1996, airport jobs in Atlanta were plentiful because of the extra business created by the summer Olympics. Instead, he strolls from shoe-shine stand to shoe-shine stand, asking, "Need anything?" He knows, as a former worker in such stands, that when business is good operators don't dare leave the stand shorthanded, so they'll pay someone a good fee to get supplies or food for them.

Or I'd tell you about Stanley Fukuda, an ex–construction worker who didn't finish college and whose building career was ended by an accident on the job that left him bedridden for eight months with a broken vertebra. His vocational rehabilitation counselors recommended that he study computers, but his own sense of what we've been calling his D.A.T.A. convinced him that bartending would be better. He paid his own way through a class on that subject.

Today Fukuda works at the Cafe Mars in San Francisco, where a *Wall Street Journal* account of his day's work makes it clear that it goes beyond the job descriptions that are written into union bartender contracts. He prepares the ingredients for the night's drinks, he supervises workers creating a drain for a new bar on the patio, he phones in orders for supplies, he reviews the bills and makes a list of the checks the cafe's owner needs to write, he sets up schedules for his coworkers on the computer, he deals with the OSHA inspector (and the health inspector and the IRS), he figures out a weekly music schedule (Tuesday, soul; Wednesday, acid jazz . . .), he finds and hires a new bouncer, he organizes a softball league for restaurant workers, he charms the customers and makes the Cafe Mars an enjoyable nightspot. And besides wages, he clears $200 in tips on a busy night.

As these cases make clear, the "marketing" that I am talking about simply involves understanding the world that you are part of and what it takes to meet its unmet needs. This marketing looks complicated only when you see it going on in a world that you do not know well. Well . . . there *is* one more situation that makes it complicated: if you are willing to work only when someone will hand you a ready-made job. That Desire used to be an Asset, since organizations were looking for people who would do what they were told and nothing more. Today, in a rapidly changing environment where the work won't stay still long enough to be pinned down in a job description, it is a debit.

HOW DO YOU IDENTIFY YOUR POTENTIAL MARKETS?

Since markets are always specific to particular situations, there is no way to list them all. But go through the following ten areas where you are most likely to find a market, keeping your own situation in mind as you do so:

1. The particular group, site, department, or team within the organization you work for, if you're currently employed. This is the obvious market for most people, since employees can hardly help knowing their own part of their organization pretty well.

2. The organization you work for as a whole. If it is fairly small, you may know your whole organization as well as a worker at a big organization would know number 1 above.

3. Some other part of your organization. Remember how your friend over in the department across the hall keeps talking about the terrible time they're having with . . . whatever? Your natural network of connections acquaints you with the problems being encountered throughout your organization. This market may be especially important if your particular area is being hit by cutbacks.

4. Some previous organization you've worked for, in part or whole. Maybe you left because of the mess they were in. Or perhaps, on the other hand, you didn't work there. Perhaps you were a student there or a regular customer of theirs. In any case, you had a pretty good idea of something they lacked and needed. This market may be particularly appropriate if you no longer have a job.

5. The industry that your present organization (or one you worked for in the past) belongs to—the computer-chip business, advertising, churches, libraries, the papermaking industry. Perhaps the problems aren't unique to your particular company or hospital or

government agency but are shared by all the organizations in this category.

6. Your own profession or trade. You work for an auto maker or a university, but you are an internal auditor or a director of communications or a maintenance person. Your market may cut across many organizations and be made up of the people who do some particular task or who belong to some functional category in those very different organizations.

7. Your community. Your market need not be work-related, of course. Look around wherever you live. The town where you live or work constitutes a market, with all kinds of unmet needs for things to be built or fixed or created, as do the individuals who live or work in the town. These needs go beyond physical ones. What type of service or what kind of a social institution does your community (or some segment of it) need?

8. Some group, community, or organization you know about. Perhaps you read a story in the paper, and it struck you that "they need help" or "there ought to be a program to work on that." What was that market?

9. Individuals like you. This one is easy to overlook because it isn't defined with a name like a company or a social institution. But if you, individually, have unmet needs, the chances are that others like you do too. And it is a market you know well, isn't it? (Remember how I got my start in this market with my first conference for teachers who—like me—were unhappy with their work.)

10. The mass market. This is what people usually mean when they say "the market" but for two reasons it often isn't the best market to start with. First, most people don't know it very well, and the whole approach we are taking to finding work is that you must know the unmet needs in your market. The second difficulty with this market is that it puts you in direct competition with sophisticated companies and sharp entrepreneurs who have researched the heck out of this market. But I don't want to try to talk you out of going for it if you have a great idea. Just be sure that the market has the needs you think it does and that you can meet them.

There may be other markets that might hold potential for you, places or groups of people that you know well. So consider this list useful only to get you thinking.

IDENTIFYING UNMET NEEDS

Finding your market is only your first step. A market is not just a collection of people; it is also a collection of unmet needs that are constantly changing as the economic, technical, regulatory, and demographic forces around it change. In any market, you need to be able to recognize the unmet needs. These needs may not even be known to the people who have them, especially if they can be filled only by a product or service that does not yet exist. In that sense, the unmet need is flagged only by a vague dissatisfaction or a limit to what can be done. Ironically, it is only the appearance on the scene of a solution that turns the situation into a "problem" that could be solved.

Whatever market you choose, there will always be specific signs that an unmet need exists in it. As with the markets themselves, such needs are countless, but they tend to be accompanied by certain typical markers. So here are some of the "flags" to look for:

1. A missing piece in a pattern or sequence. This is the classic "breakthrough" situation, for when the piece is found everything falls into place. But people may not even realize that the piece is missing, because the underlying pattern or sequence is not yet clear in their minds. So you may need to do a good deal of conceptual activity and communication to educate the market about the total pattern from which the piece is missing. I myself capitalized on one such missing piece when, early in my consulting career, I realized that there were lots of consulting and training services that helped organizations make changes, but few that helped employees deal with the psychological impact of the change on them.

2. An unrecognized opportunity. This occurs when the situation that an individual or an organization is in changes. All it takes is someone to see what could be done, and people say, "Why didn't we do that long ago?" You might find such a situation where your organization's customers had a need that wasn't being filled.

3. An underused resource. This situation occurs when something that an individual or an organization could capitalize on isn't being used. Maybe it's because of rigid thinking, or maybe it's because no one sees how to apply the resource in question, but when the "answer" appears, success can follow very quickly. Restaurants, for example, have long had more capacity to prepare meals than to serve them to seated guests. But until recently, few but specialty shops prepared food for take-out or delivery.

4. A "signal event"—especially an unexpected success or failure. We like to think that we pick up on the cues that life sends to signal us that things are different now. Unfortunately, when they take the form of an unexpected success or an unexpected failure, we often miss them because we are so pleased with the success or so distressed at the failure. We are too caught up in our reaction to notice the cue. Actually, the failure may be saying, "It wasn't your fault; it's just that that way of doing things is becoming passé"; and the success may be saying, "Don't be so delighted with your windfall that you fail to notice that you got it by doing something you never tried before."

5. An unacknowledged change. Changes often happen gradually and can take a long time to be understood, even by the people most affected by them. This is especially true of "paradigm shifts," in which a whole way of seeing things dissolves and another way takes its place. Such a shift totally redefines the unmet needs of the affected area. A whole range of products and services for families with two careers or one working parent falls into this category. The demographics changed and so did the needs, but business continued to think of "families" as though all the mothers stayed at home.

6. An "impossible" situation. These situations are so bad that people stop looking at them as unmet needs or even as problems to be solved. Instead they see them as horrible, endlessly frustrating, and hopeless conditions that you have to live with or steer around. But they are unmet needs, with a huge payoff for whoever can find a way to meet them. The early copying machines continually needed servicing, and people grew accustomed to this frustrating reality— until Canon began to produce copiers that almost never malfunctioned. (As so often happens, the other companies didn't have

much "desire" to solve this problem, because they were making good money from the repair business.)

7. A nonexistent-but-needed service. The symptoms of such a need are persistent frustration, the existence of a complicated set of procedures to avoid the problem, or constant discussion about "there oughta be a (something or other)." A brainstorming session often brings ideas for needed services to the surface. If you've ever had a serious illness for an extended period of time, for example, you know that there ought to be a better way for doctors and institutions to share information about you than shipping or having you hand-carry hard copies and films of the information about you. Those get lost. They don't arrive in time for your appointment. Copying takes time. It's a nightmare for the patient, and it drives medical personnel crazy too.

8. A new or emerging problem. There is always a time lag between the appearance of a difficulty and a recognition of it for what it is. That gap is full of unfocused grumbling and repeated attempts to make the old way work. It's a time when the ability to frame the problem, to put it into words, or to give it a name can pay off handsomely. All the problems associated with managing, rewarding, evaluating, and organizing a dejobbed workforce. Hey, maybe *that's* the market you have been looking for.

9. A roadblock, a bottleneck, a shortage, a limitation, or a chronic weakness. The problems that occur again and again drive everyone crazy. The larger system may be quite adequate, but "there's this one bottleneck where everything slows to a crawl." "We keep running short of this item." "We get things just so far, and then we run into a wall." "We are just inherently weak in this particular area over here." OK, you've just been given the unmet-need signal. To draw on my own experience again, the moment I remember was when a manager said, "We have to change, but everyone is so busy defending the importance of his job that . . ." (I never heard the rest of the sentence, because the implications of the statement were reverberating through my mind.)

10. An interface between groups that have different values, languages, or outlooks. Whether it is between the organization and its cus-

tomers, the regular workers and the temps, or the internal operations and the outsourced ones, modern organizations are full of "interfaces" where communication breaks down. Every one of them is the site of numerous unmet needs. As formerly integrated activities or functions get unbundled, boundaries multiply, so this is an unmet need that is guaranteed to grow in the years ahead.

As you read over these signs, think of others in the markets you know well. Think of how the unmet needs in your own life show up and how their existence is signaled by situations or feelings or behaviors. Mentally add your own "flags" to the ten given above.

MARKETING AND "MARKETING YOURSELF"

"I don't know how to market myself." Some version of that lament is common to most people whose careers have thus far been job-based. I know. I felt exactly that way for the first half-dozen years after I left my job as a college teacher in 1974. Worse, I even thought of "marketing" oneself as just a step up from prostitution. (It was "selling" yourself, wasn't it?) It meant that you had to forget your own values and do whatever people wanted you to, didn't it? You had to learn to dumb down everything you did to the lowest common denominator and turn the whole thing into a sales pitch, didn't you?

The answers to these questions are no, no, and no, respectively. Marketing isn't "selling"—not that there is anything wrong with selling. Rather, it is a three-stage process.

1. You identify the unmet needs of various groups and institutions in your marketplace and find which, if any, correspond to the resources you have to offer.

2. You combine the unmet needs you have identified with the D.A.T.A. you have to offer into a *product* that both capitalizes on your resources and confers appreciable benefits on your customer.

3. You draw from your understanding of both the unmet needs and your D.A.T.A. to make an effective case for your product's meeting the unmet needs in question.

At this point, the "selling" is expressing what is authentic to you (as guaranteed by your D.A.T.A.) and will meet a genuine need that your customer has. Nothing sleazy about that!

The second and third stages of marketing are the subject of Chapter 8, and the selling of the final product will be covered in Chapter 9. For now, the essential thing for you to do is survey the markets that are available to you and discover what their unmet needs are. Until you have done that, you will lack a viable product. And in a dejobbed world, a worker without a product is like a company without a product: full of potential resources, perhaps, but competitively not even in the game. That would be a shame, for this basic stage of marketing is as straightforward and doable as it is important. The steps may be unfamiliar to you, but they are hardly difficult to learn.

IDENTIFYING YOUR MARKETS AND THEIR NEEDS

Step One

Particularize the markets by filling in the following list. Item A, for example, asks for "your particular group, site, department, or team." Which is it going to be? Which of them is the market where you can see needs that are going unmet? Item B refers to your organization as a whole—is that practical? You need to get down to particulars.

A. The particular group, site, department, or team within the organization you work for:

———————————————————————————————

———————————————————————————————

B. The organization you work for as a whole:

———————————————————————————————

———————————————————————————————

C. Some other part of your organization:

———————————————————————————————

———————————————————————————————

D. Some previous organization you've worked for, in part or in whole:

_____

_____

E. The industry or public area that your present (or past) organization is in:

_____

_____

F. Your own individual profession or trade:

_____

_____

G. Your community:

_____

_____

H. Some group, community, or organization you know about:

_____

_____

I. Individuals like you:

_____

_____

J. The mass market:

_____

_____

Step Two

Now identify unmet needs that you've spotted in the last year. Remember to be particular. Item 1 on this list asks for "a missing piece in a pattern or sequence." Fine, but what pattern or sequence? Here are some examples:

- the process of filling orders where you used to work
- how a new family finds out about and enrolls its children in school
- how a new skill required by a government agency leads to a course teaching that skill to the people who need it

Imagine one example of each of these unmet needs:

1. A missing piece in a pattern or sequence:

_____

_____

2. An unrecognized opportunity:

_____

_____

3. An underused resource:

_____

_____

4. A signal event—an unexpected success or failure:

_____

_____

5. An unacknowledged change:

_____

_____

6. An "impossible" situation:

_____

_____

7. A nonexistent-but-needed service:

_____

_____

8. A new or emerging problem:

_____

_____

9. A roadblock, a bottleneck, a shortage, a limitation or a chronic weakness:

_____

_____

10. An interface between different groups:

_____

_____

Step Three

The following grid puts these two lists together. Think of the intersections between the two lists—as represented by the grid on the next page. Put an X in the blocks where a particular unmet need and a particular context fit together: if you are aware of an "underused resource" (3) in "your community" (G), for example, put an X in box G3. Mark all the boxes that represent items that you could provide an example for.

	A	B	C	D	E	F	G	H	I	J
1										
2										
3										
4										
5										
6										
7										
8										
9										
10										

Step Four

Wherever in the grid you have an X, you have a potential opportunity. *Viable* opportunities for You & Co. exist only where the need coincides with your D.A.T.A., of course. From the X-marked squares, choose three that look interesting to you, and describe each one briefly below.

Opportunity One:

_____

_____

_____

Opportunity Two:

_____

_____

_____

Opportunity Three:

_____

_____

_____

CONCLUSION

This marketing approach to finding work may show you that you need to learn more about your potential customers and their unmet needs than you know now. Even if those needs are just down the hall at the place where you work, your job-centered attitude may well keep you from seeing them. Don't feel embarrassed about that ignorance, though. It is simply a by-product of an outlook that you had to have to get hired to do a job, to get good evaluations for how you did your job, and to get raises for doing a good job. No wonder you are job-centered!

The "marketing imagination" that will be necessary to succeed in the job-free world of tomorrow is something that you can start developing immediately. You need to imagine that you are a detective on a case, or a writer on a research project, or a consultant trying to figure out what's wrong with a company, or a student trying to learn a new subject. (Choose your metaphor, or create another for the investigative outlook that such a marketer needs to have.) You need to ask and listen and think from new perspectives.

Six months of such investigation, and you will know a lot about your potential market(s) that you don't know now. Presuming that you are lucky enough to be presently employed, use that employment as a kind of "student aid" to carry you while you learn. If you aren't employed, you may want to go out and find a job to see you through your period of study. But whatever you do to cover the rent and the grocery bills, you need to be figuring out how your market(s) work and what unmet needs exist in it (them).

Books on job hunting tell you to "network." It is true that the people who do best at marketing have good networks. But the sad fact is that the people who do best already had good networks *before they needed them.* That's important to remember for two reasons:

1. It reminds you to get going on this project. Now. Even though your job is "pretty secure." Now is the time to be talking with others, either in the organizations that interest you or in the profession or trade you mean to practice.

2. When you don't have the network in place, they tell you to do "informational interviews." There are a couple of problems with such interviews. The first is that the people who know about opportunities are usually overloaded with requests for such interviews. The second is that when you are really, in your heart, hoping to be offered a job, you'll tip your hand without even realizing it. "This is just an informational interview. I am not asking if you know of any jobs! Really! (Incidentally, do you?)" You may never express that parenthetical question openly, but it seeps out of the cracks of what you say. Then people feel manipulated and don't want to help you.

So you have to set up your investigations as a multisided project. Keep that larger project in mind whenever you talk to anyone about work. The project will include the following activities:

- Not only formal "interviews," but all the chance conversations you have in which the topic of work comes up.
- Reading the daily press and work-related publications. You probably ought to start cutting out stories or jotting down information as you come across it. Schedule a little library time to check out which are the best periodicals for the market(s) you have chosen.
- Visits to potential client sites to gain firsthand impressions of what's needed. You should also pick up anything about the client that you can legally get your hands on and read it carefully.

The point is that you need to *know* your client in a way that you never had to know your employer. You are looking for unmet needs. In the job world, it was the employer's responsibility to translate those unmet needs into tasks, assign some of them to existing employees, and then turn the remainder into "job requisitions," which later became "job openings."

But waiting for that to happen and then applying just doesn't cut it any more. For one thing, the employer is trying to cut costs and so doesn't want to hire any more full-time, long-term employees. For another thing, some insider always hears about the job requisition before it turns into an opening and alerts a friend to it. And finally, the approach of focusing on the "job" misses what it is that the client is really looking for anyway: a solution to a specific, unmet need. The client is really looking for a "product" of some kind. How to combine your D.A.T.A. and your market information into a product is the subject of the next chapter.

CHAPTER EIGHT

Creating Your Product

*It is not the employer who pays wages—he only handles the money. It is the
product that pays wages.*

—Henry Ford

Why You Had Better Have a "Product"

When I wrote *JobShift,* I included two pages on creating your "product." In
that general analysis, the subject was secondary. But in this guide the subject of product creation is central, because it is this product that your
client is buying. To say that you are "looking for a job" is to slip out of the
orbit of our dejobbed age, because what you are really doing is selling the
client a product.

There has been a huge shift in the opportunity structure of our economy,
and the present location of opportunity is (as we saw in the last chapter)
in the unmet needs of clients. As big organizations are being unbundled,
many of the clients you will be serving are the managers and executives of
those organizations, who used to have their needs met by regular employees. Or they are the managers and leaders at the unbundled pieces of
formerly big organizations, who now lack the staff to do everything in-
house. In either case, clients are more and more likely to go outside their
own organizations to fill their needs.

But you must understand what these clients are looking for. They aren't
looking for "good candidates," "well-trained professionals," "experienced
workers," or any of the other staples of the job application process. These

clients are looking for solutions to their problems and answers to their needs. They are, to put it simply, looking for "products." These clients are looking for products even (no, *especially*) when times are so hard that there isn't a "job" to be had for miles around.

Yet when I ask most people what their "product" is, I get into a confused and confusing exchange similar to the frustrating miscommunication that can cloud the issue of one's market. Here's one example:

"You mean the company's product?" the manager asked.

"No, I mean yours," I replied.

"Well, I'm in Personnel," she said.

"Great. Good field. What's your product?"

"I am a compensation-and-benefits specialist."

"Interesting role. But what's your *product*?"

"Compensation and benefits," she said hopefully, but I could tell from her questioning tone that she didn't get the point.

"That's not really a product," I replied. "A product is something that somebody buys. It represents a solution to a problem, it confers an advantage, it meets a need, it exploits a possibility. Comp-and-benefit systems are just organizational furniture."

"No they aren't. They motivate people, they communicate priorities, they help people to support their families, they embody the psychological contract between the company and its workers!" (You can tell that this manager really knows and believes in the value of her work.)

"Now you're getting warm. The company needs to reward its workers for all those reasons. So a comp-and-benefits system is necessary, and that justifies your department. But what justifies you? What do (or could) you deliver that would make it worthwhile to pay you money every week? What can you do that would make them say of your pay, 'Boy, *that's* money well spent! Did that person ever add value to what our customers get for their money!'"

You can see where a conversation like this is headed, although I have to admit that even when it has come this far, it can still be a long time before it reaches its logical outcome. The difficulty is that although organizations talk a lot about "value-added activities" and "making sure that everything we do benefits our customers," people really cannot *get* those ideas until they give up the picture of themselves as people who have been hired to "do their jobs."

Telling people about this isn't really going to change their perceptions either; all that people hear is that their jobs had better contribute to the final benefit that the customer receives—or they'll lose them. It's jobs, jobs, jobs! But there is a change under way, not because someone is pushing it or because the CEO wants it or because government regulations encourage it, or because consultants like me are talking about it.

The change is driven by the six forces that we identified in Chapter 1:

1. *Knowledge work*—which is far harder to divide up into conventional long-term jobs than the physical work of the industrial era was and far more likely to need workers who are grouped into short-lived, cross-functional teams. Knowledge work also has short production runs and product cycles, both of which make fixed organizational arrangements a handicap.

2. *Communications and information technology*—which makes the knowledge work possible but also allows the organization to disperse its workers, separate the groups working on related tasks, and allocate tasks to groups that are not even part of the organization. The communications and information technology also accelerates the pace of change that the organization must deal with.

3. *The speed of change*—which is both an effect and a cause of the two items above, requires organizations to abandon whatever slows down the cycle that begins with identifying the customer need; goes through the design, production, and distribution of a product; and ends with further services for a satisfied customer.

4. *Management responses to increased competition*—everything from reengineering to TQM to empowered and cross-trained teams. Every one of these efforts piles new changes atop the old changes and further erodes the outlines of the traditional job.

5. *The unbundling of the organization*—all of the factors flow, like tributaries into a swelling river, into the tendency to break up the traditional, integrated organization into its component activities and to link those activities more loosely than ever before. Some of those unbundled elements are then turned over to workers who are not full-time, long-term employees.

6. *The market created by the baby boom*—which has elevated the demand for individualized, immediate, and value-added products, all of which require the kinds of work described above. Further, due to their "free agent" mentality, baby boomers tend to be willing to launch out on their own and, even when employed, to find the constraints of the traditional job more onerous than their parents did.

Having tracked the forces at work in today's workplace this far, we can now say that it isn't just that jobs slow things down. It is that jobs neither maximize the benefits of the new organization nor fit its needs. For just as the new organization is externally "market driven" to a much greater degree than its predecessors were, it is also internally "market driven."

To serve its own internal market, the postindustrial organization needs not loyal employees (who don't even understand that the organization is a market), but committed, market-minded suppliers of whatever products and services the organization needs. That is why I am arguing that the person who wishes to build a career around serving such an organization must forget about a job and create, instead, a product that meets one of the organization's specific and pressing needs.

WHY "PRODUCT"? WHY NOT "SERVICE"?

The reason that I keep using the term "product" is that markets—especially the internal market—favor products. Most organizations prefer the transactional style of a product, in which input is transformed into output and people have to pay for what they get. Products fill niches created by unmet needs and are easy to sell or purchase as needed. They are easy to budget for. They are simple to justify on a cost-benefit basis.

Many employees would prefer to talk about the "services" that they render their employer, but there are several reasons why that term is not so useful:

- Services are diffuse and readily come unstuck from the unmet need that they should be serving.
- Service is an inherently conservative concept that is less likely to change with a changing situation than a product is. The world of

products naturally connotes innovation and changing business arrangements.

■ It's harder and less common to advocate or question services on a cost-benefit basis because they're less crisply defined than products.

■ Services appeal more to the private preferences of the client than do products, which are likely to be more directly related to some identifiable organizational need.

These things make the value of services to the organization harder to determine by objective standards.

I don't deny the utility of the conventional distinction between product-making organizations and service delivery organizations. We should note, however, that that distinction is becoming pretty slippery, as computer companies discover that "delivering MIS services" is their *product,* and HMOs compete on the basis of whose health care *product* better serves the needs of the buyer.

On the worker's side, defining what one sells as a product imposes more discipline on the seller than defining it as a service does. The word *product* inherently leads one to think of benefits to the client, advantages over rival products, and the relation between the price charged and the value added. Terming the individual's output a "product" fits the new idea of the individual as a micro-organization, a little You & Co. that is subject to the same forces and constraints as big organizations are. In other words, converting "working" into "supplying a product" helps to educate us about the realities of the world in which our clients exist.

HOW CHANGE CREATES PRODUCT OPPORTUNITIES

We've already pointed out that change creates new opportunities as it destroys old ones. This process can be seen clearly whenever an industry is hit by a sudden event that changes how business is done.

Such an event happened several years ago in the travel industry. Travel agents had lived on the edge of the rapidly changing world of tourism and airlines travel for decades without changing the basic elements of a fairly standardized service (and I mean "service," not "product") for which they were paid the time-honored 10 percent commission. In 1995, Delta Air Lines changed that business by announcing that it would no longer pay that commission; it would, instead, pay flat fees of $25 (one way) and $50 (round trip) on domestic tickets. Other airlines, pushed by competition and rising costs, quickly followed suit. And overnight, the market in which the travel agents operated changed dramatically.

Most travel agencies reacted as individual employees do when the rules of the employment game change dramatically. They yelled bloody murder, they started looking for ways to economize, and they held on for dear life in hopes that their competitors would fold first. But some travel agencies took the new situation as a message of a very different kind: a signal that it was time to stop delivering a fairly conventional service and create, instead, distinct products to meet particular unmet needs. The results were various and fascinating.

- Travelfest redefined its product and its venue. No longer was the product tickets and the venue a travel agency. Now the venue was a store and the product was anything a traveler might need for a trip, such as water purifiers, visa applications, books on trekking, classes in everything from speaking Spanish to dealing with a flying phobia, and (of course) tickets.
- Aspen Travel redefined the product in a different way. This agency chose the market of movie production companies and redefined its product as everything that market might need, like "how to get an AT&T booth to a location in Belize—or how to transport penguins to Moab, Utah, without having them collapse from heatstroke . . . [or how to] accommodate a last-minute destination change for a crew of 20."
- PC Travel redefined the product in a different way, by making the way the customer interfaced with the company so different that everything changed. Instead of the ticket being something that you went out to buy, like a loaf of bread, PC Travel put the whole reservation-making, ticket-issuing process on the Internet. The company now has 70,000 registered users engaging in electronic commerce, not retail shopping.

The reason I have illustrated my argument with organizational examples rather than individual ones is that the whole relationship between vendor and client and the critical role in it that a well-defined product plays are easier to see in that more familiar marketing context. But remember, you are a micro-organization yourself now. Almost anything you offer to an organizational client will be in competition with something offered by some other (if you will, "real") organization. So you may as well get used to thinking in those terms. Besides, these examples help you to see the relevance of the dozens of examples that you can find every week in the business press.

ENVISIONING THE MARKET

As you begin to think of how you are going to develop your product, you need to remember how important it is to envision your market clearly and distinctively. People talk about making your organization or yourself different, but they often fail to note that such "differentiating" is simply cosmetic if it is not based on a distinct view of the market. Such skin-deep differentiation is, in fact, what gives the concept of "repositioning" yourself in the market its reputation of being a verbal "spin" that doesn't really change anything. But really envisioning a different market has profound and lasting results.

Let's imagine that you decide that your D.A.T.A. makes a personally relevant product very appealing to you. You also hope that you can turn your being an African-American woman into an Asset. You want your product to be something that "improves" the world (Desire). You are good at explaining things, particularly at getting people to see things from a new point of view (Ability). Your Temperament lends itself to interpersonal work, learning, and group activity.

So you decide that your product is going to be a training program in diversity. Not only does it fit your D.A.T.A., but almost everyone understands that organizations need help with diversity-related problems. So far, so good. But here (as often) you will need to revisit the marketing issue a second time to differentiate the product enough to address it to a need that is both recognizable and still unmet. In this case, whom, specifically, is that diversity program for?

- Is it for a whole world or a whole nation that needs to learn to live successfully with its otherwise divisive differences?
- Is it for executives who are starting to recognize that their organizations will be damaged if they are hit by highly publicized lawsuits?

- Is it for fairly traditionally minded team leaders, who now desperately need to learn how to unlock and use the talents of the very diverse teams that they lead?
- Is it for individually unique employees, who need to learn how to contribute to a common effort and still be true to themselves?

Now let's imagine that this project idea began when you heard the rumor that your old company was interested in setting up "diversity training." What you probably didn't hear was which of the above groups it was for. And maybe the company itself didn't know yet. That is where you have some work to do: one of the tasks that dejobbing imposes upon the individual worker is to collaborate with the client on defining the task to be done. Until you establish the audience, you aren't going to have a product to sell. You'll just be peddling a panacea, a "cure for whatever ails you," and your chances of success will be small.

YOU DON'T HAVE TO CHOOSE A CUTTING-EDGE FIELD

Norm Brodsky is an entrepreneur who has started a number of successful small businesses, and he says that his first criterion for choosing the market he wants to enter is "a concept that's been around for 100 years or more." Having said that, he admits that he doesn't literally mean a full century but that his point is that it should be "an established concept, one that everybody understands. It's not new and revolutionary." Why? "Because there is nothing more expensive than educating a market."

You don't need to agree with Brodsky's preference for products that customers can recognize as beneficial on day one. I myself haven't followed that rule. My own D.A.T.A. is such that I enjoy and work well in markets that aren't yet fully understood by either their component customers or by other product providers. I think they're exciting. I no sooner begin to write about our not-yet-articulated diversity program than I start imagining how I'd sell executives and managers on its importance. All the same, Brodsky's right. Educating your market to recognize itself as a market takes time, energy, new ideas, and a tolerance for slow results. And money doesn't hurt.

The economy is full of successful products that the client or customer didn't recognize as beneficial until after they were created: the Dodge minivan and the Sony Walkman were both dismissed as uninteresting by focus groups of customers in the early stages of their development. One can imagine the reactions: "Let's see if I have it straight. You are going to make a hi-fi unit that people can wear around their waists? Won't that be heavy? Just a little bigger than a cigarette pack? Hey, I want to hear music, not static!"

Norm Brodsky's second criterion for a new business is even more useful for the dejobbed worker to think about: "I want [a work situation] that is antiquated. I don't necessarily mean 'old-fashioned.' I'm talking about a business in which most of [your competition is] out of step with the customer." Often this means heading for the parts of your market that have lagged behind the changes that have been made elsewhere—the back-office operations, for example, of a company that has raced ahead of the pack in its marketing and customer service areas.

But the same behind-the-curve situation can exist where (and because) your client's part of the organization has moved forward more quickly than the rest. For whenever one part of an organization gets out in front of the crowd, the interfaces between it and the rest of the organization are sure to be problem areas, full of misunderstanding, cross-purposes, and needs that are not only unmet but not even described yet.

Brodsky's final criterion for a business that's worth starting is the existence of a *niche*, which corresponds in our terms to a very well defined unmet need. He uses the example of one of his own start-ups, a records storage company called CitiStorage. Most records storage companies were just places to park old files. Getting into those files, if the need arose, was so difficult that organizations sometimes gave up trying, even when they really needed to get the information. The only exceptions to the park-em-and-forget-em strategy were two huge, technically sophisticated facilities that were so far away in the countryside that companies felt cut off from their records.

Brodsky's "niche" was a city-based, technically sophisticated facility, where records could be stacked many boxes deep but still retrieved quickly with the aid of automated machinery. In our terms, we'd say that he found an unmet need in the market and devised a product to meet it. Not too surprisingly, CitiStorage has been very successful.

Not only can your product be in a fairly traditional field, it can actually represent a backward turn of the clock, whereby you return to something that used to be important but then got lost along the way. Take Black Oak Books, an independent bookstore in Berkeley, California. Its market is the sophisticated readers and researchers of that university town, and it built its reputation originally as a place to find good used and hard-to-locate books.

It shifted its focus over the years, however, leaving behind that product and becoming simply a good, neighborhood source for new books. The work was easier, it required less knowledge, and the product turned considerably faster. But then the big national chains—with their discount prices, their megastores, and their oversized advertising budgets—entered Black Oak's market. Red ink started to flow. After a difficult period of self-study, Black Oak reversed its direction and went back to a heavy reliance on its former product: used books. The results have been quite successful. It has cut its debts by half and has turned worsening losses into consistent and growing profits.

In a society as innovation-oriented as ours, people (and companies) are quick to abandon products whose total market size is shrinking. But such shrinking markets may provide very solid opportunities for committed producers because of what is sometimes called the "last iceman" phenomenon. Obviously, ice delivery isn't the business it was in the day of iceboxes, but when the number of suppliers dwindles to one, he or she gets all the business there is—and that may be a significant amount. That's why, for example, there are still thriving manufacturers of buggy whips and radio vacuum tubes!

THE INDIVIDUAL PATH TO A PRODUCT

It's instructive to track this product-inventing process in the life of a single, dejobbed worker. Take William Gibson, who is presently an executive, but who began his quest for a product with a college job as a newspaper delivery truck driver. Although it was a long time before that experience proved to be an asset with any relevance to the rest of his D.A.T.A., his experience and fascination with how the *Philadelphia Inquirer* got delivered turned out to be valuable.

In the meantime, however, he became a computer programmer and then a manager of programmers. He finally worked his way up to the presidency of Scientific Timesharing, whose product was time on that company's mainframes. When that product neared the end of its life span, he began to look for another unmet need and another way to use his resources. He recognized that his company had developed the ability to track highly complex interactions, like the accumulated time spent using a computer, and he looked for a market that needed such a resource. Wal-Mart and other retailers were parlaying their need to reduce inventory into a computer-based, real-time link between distributors and stores called Electronic Data Interchange (EDI). Leaving Scientific Timeshare and starting a software supplier called Manugistics, Gibson adapted his technology to the EDI market and became Wal-Mart's EDI supplier. On the basis of that success, he soon had fourteen of the country's biggest grocery chains as his customers too.

More recently, by responding to another unmet need, he has managed to more than double Manugistics's business revenues between 1993 and 1996. The new need: manufacturing companies that want to increase the speed with which they turn materials into products and orders into deliveries by avoiding kinks and gaps in the supply chain. This is where Gibson's experience as a delivery van driver turned into an asset. Timken Steel has used Manugistics to get 15 percent more output from its existing facilities at a tiny fraction of the $20 to $30 million they would have had to spend on expanding their facilities to secure the same gain. This new technology is what the research director at one of the country's biggest computer consultancies calls "the superhot computing area in corporate America now."

Gibson's experience illustrates why I keep calling the output of the de-jobbed worker a *product*. Gibson's software offers a service, but in this world where things are purchased by people looking for gains in speed and decreases in cost, those things are most easily discussed as product benefits. And that fact takes us one further step in our discussion: you need to create a product, but what you will really be selling is not the product but the benefits that it provides. To do so, you need to understand the specific uses to which your product will be put. I emphasize again: study your market and its unmet needs! Then you can present your product to your client as *solutions to specific problems*.

YOUR OWN PRODUCT DEVELOPMENT

At a conference in New Jersey, I heard an outplacement executive talk about her own career change in terms of a discovered product. She had been marketing manager for Nabisco's Chips Ahoy, but her real desire was to work in financial services. In her mind, however, she saw herself as a cookie person—or did, until she realized that her product was really the capacity to create a market for something new—not just a new cookie, but anything new. With that discovery, she began presenting herself very differently to prospective clients and employers and ended up as the marketing manager for a new stock fund. In the course of her presentation at the conference, she emphasized how much job titles distract us from the product we can deliver to a client. She illustrated her point by saying that file clerks keep getting jobs as . . . file clerks. But if they can see themselves as experts in "information retrieval," a whole new world of opportunity opens before them.

The great philosopher William James said that "genius means little more than the faculty of perceiving in an unhabitual way." The first file clerk who went into the information retrieval business was that kind of a genius. And like other geniuses, she or he was probably pooh-poohed by people who didn't understand what the newly christened "information retriever" was talking about.

If you are faced with such incomprehension, just remind yourself:

- The Beatles' first audition for a commercial recording company came to nothing when they were told by a recording executive that "guitar groups are on the way out."
- In 1968 *Business Week* dismissed Japanese cars with the statement, "With fifteen types of foreign cars already on sale here, the Japanese auto industry isn't likely to carve out a big share of the market for itself."

These examples of blindness, like those of people that you may encounter as you develop your own product, do not necessarily come from stupidity or maliciousness. The people who dismiss your ideas simply fail to understand how change affects markets and creates needs that can be filled by people who know how to turn their D.A.T.A. into a product.

"PRODUCTS" AREN'T JUST FOR ENTREPRENEURS

The way to create a product is easiest to illustrate with the examples of independent workers who have already separated themselves from a job and who consider themselves independent. Remember, however, that their most important independence is a state of mind, rather than an actual life situation.

I was doing some training at a NASA facility recently, and one of the seminar participants, Jill, was a former human resources specialist who had recognized that the NASA budget was shrinking and that her department was likely to face job cuts. She had a natural ease with computers and a desire to do something more creative. Having done some training in the past, she was aware how seldom training materials are really well designed.

As Jill watched the first belt tightening take place, she could see that people without a clear contribution to make were going to be at risk. She took stock of her assets and decided that she needed a little more training in instructional design, so she signed up for a course at a local college. Then she put together a proposal for NASA: that she become a one-stop shop for anyone at the site who needed help putting together the visual support for presentations, courses, and meetings.

Jill's product met an unmet need, because such work had previously been done haphazardly by employees without much skill or training, or by outside vendors who charged a lot for the service. Her proposal was accepted, and she now runs a little in-house shop, turning out a product as though she were an independent vendor but still on the payroll as an employee.

I came across another person who operated just *outside* the employee-contractor divide but had done something very similar. Arthur's product was coaching for consultants who were having difficulty with client projects, and he was retained by a very large consulting firm on a full-time basis. He was sitting in a seminar I ran at the consulting firm, and I would not have known that he wasn't an employee if he hadn't told me.

Arthur was an independent consultant and Jill was an employee, but neither one was what those terms meant before organizations began to dejob their work. Both had learned the secret of market analysis and both understood just what it was that they had to offer. Neither one had a job in the old sense; both had a clear product.

This kind of career need not be limited to a single role, for it can lead to further products and positions. An employee at a New York–based clothing company has made her way up the organizational ladder by identifying, in one situation after another, work that needed to be done and then (if it matched her resources) suggesting that she take it on. "I've created nearly every job I've had," she told an interviewer. Her own experience has led to something approaching a policy, because she then added, "We promote from within not just to positions that exist but to jobs that people create." She is now, incidentally, the CEO of the company, so this approach does not need to damage your career prospects.

I want to make clear, with these examples, that dejobbing and the need to know what your product is will be important to you not only if and when you decide to operate *outside* the organization. Inside and out don't make nearly the difference they once did. Not only are similar tasks performed by people on both sides of that line, and not only do similar strategies serve people on both sides of that line well, but is also likely that you will cross that line several times during the rest of your career. You'll operate for a while as an employee, and then you'll go off on your own, perhaps returning to work for your old firm as a vendor. You'll be on your own for a while, and then you'll join with other independents to work in some new little organization. But then you'll be hired by one of your client firms and work as their employee for a while. *In* and *out,* it won't make much difference.

Whatever your nominal situation at any given time, you'll be a worker with a product. And you'll need to manage yourself, in or out, as a little business. By a lucky coincidence, the next chapter is about how to put all this together in You & Co. Before we leave our present subject, however, let's make sure that you have the product development process clear.

HOW TO START DESIGNING YOUR PRODUCT

Method One

Review your D.A.T.A. (see Part II of this book) and the unmet needs or unexploited possibilities in some market that you know well (see the grid at the end of Chapter 7). Where do those intersect? It's wherever those intersections match the resources your D.A.T.A. provide you with that you can create a marketable product.

This isn't easy. But remember that any time you spend on your D.A.T.A. and your market(s) produces knowledge that can be used again and again for additional products, product extensions, and product improvements. To stumble onto a product without gaining a thorough understanding of your D.A.T.A. and your market(s) is actually a stroke of bad luck because it makes you feel that you know more about what you are doing than you actually do.

Remember that a product *is not*

- what you do at work or what you could do if you had the chance
- your job description or position title
- your skill or the training you have had or the experience you bring to a project

A product *is*

- something that solves the client's problem
- something that confers a benefit on the client
- something that produces the outcome that the client wants
- something that adds value missing in other comparable products

Method Two

Imagine that you've just left your client after having delivered your product. Imagine how your client might answer these questions:

1. How have I or my situation improved since You & Co. came in the door?

2. What do I have to show for the money I paid You & Co.?

3. How can I measure the benefit of You & Co.?

4. To whom would I recommend You & Co., and why?

Method Three

Write an ad for your product in the space below. If you don't feel ready to do this now, go back and review your D.A.T.A. and your market possibilities. Whenever you're ready, *write that ad.* It is a wonderful way to assure yourself that you know what you are selling, to whom you are selling, why they should buy, and how to tell them that.

Running Your Microbusiness

The days of the mammoth corporations are coming to an end. People are going to have to create their own lives, their own careers, and their own successes. Some people may go kicking and screaming into this new world, but there is only one message there. You're now in business for yourself.

—ROBERT SCHAEN, FORMER CONTROLLER, AMERITECH

THE FUTURE OF SMALL BUSINESS

Robert Schaen, whose words provide the heading to this chapter, was a telephone executive. Then he followed his own advice: he now runs a small company that publishes children's books. Having read this far, you will hardly be surprised to find that I think he is right in saying that we are now "in business for ourselves." The last chapter was based on the assumption that you will need to get yourself a product and begin to market it as though you were a little business.

But there is another sense in which Schaen's example is a little misleading, for it suggests that you ought to go out and launch an actual company, complete with its own employees and all the paraphernalia of the corporate world. Schaen chose publishing children's books as his new company's business. Your choice would be different, of course: publishing a new magazine, running a specialty catering service, opening an antique shop, or maybe buying a franchise of some kind.

But don't go dashing out to start up your new venture. It's not that these are the wrong things to consider, but they do belong more to the age that is passing than to the age that is dawning. That is, they are small businesses in the old-fashioned sense: stand-alone operations that pick out a niche to fill in the big mass market and grow (even become big) if they are successful. That is a world in which entrepreneurs put lots of sweat-equity into their start-up businesses and then sell them for a bundle when they have established themselves.

The new world is not so much made up of these kinds of small-businesses-growing-large as it is made up of microbusinesses that are meant to be successful and lucrative but are not necessarily intended ever to become big businesses. They aren't meant to grow much because they are meant to capitalize on the opportunities of being small and simple. They are one-person *atoms,* or one-or-two-person-plus-a-couple-of-support-people *molecules.* They are not "small businesses" in the conventional sense of the mom and pop store, the little furniture refinishing business, or the suburban dentist's office.

One difference is that their market is made up of other organizations rather than of individual consumers. Even there, they are not traditional "suppliers." Rather, they provide their organizational clients with alternatives to hiring a new employee or a dozen of them. These new small businesses are not stand-alone shops and stores serving local clients, but form an integral part of a wide, loose, electronically linked organizational network that runs a new kind of "distributed" business activity. The old small businesses aspired to be big businesses. The new small businesses aspire to grow as increasingly sophisticated and successful specialty operations, not as "growing and multipurpose organizations" in the old-fashioned sense.

In the same way that many individuals are still looking for the old form of employment (the job), many people who think of starting a small business are still imagining the old form of that activity. But that path is narrowing, even as the crowd attempting to enter it is swelling. The result: roadblock. An alternative route that is much wider and freer of traffic is the world of activity that is distributed among the atoms and molecules of microbusinesses.

If you intend to join this growing area of business, there are two things that you need to understand—not as concepts but as truths that you *get* in your very bones.

- You don't need to learn how to start a small business. Instead you must recognize that *you already are* a small business and now need only learn how to act like one.
- Furthermore, that realization applies to you whether you are no longer employed in a job, not yet employed, or presently have a job in a big organization and don't want to leave. In all cases, *you already are* a small business.

As you consider "your own business," remember those facts. I am not trying to get you to quit your job or give up looking for another one. I am trying to get you to abandon the job-based mindset and to develop a microbusiness mindset instead.

WHAT BUSINESS ARE YOU IN?

What kind of business? This is the first question you'll have to answer if you're to function effectively in this new world. That question always used to refer you to what business your employer was in, but now that you are yourself a business it's *you* I'm talking about. Say, what business *are* you in, anyway?

That question is very closely related to the questions about your product that you've just been wrestling with, but it is a little more general. What is the business that your product belongs to? The short answer may take you back to the name of your old department: You're in the *training* (or purchasing, sales, or product design) business.

But those terms belong more to the old world of small business than to the new. You're not just a little training firm that may one day grow to be a big training company. You're a firm that helps companies transform their job-minded employees into vendor-minded ones. Or a business that helps companies develop a new kind of manager, who can manage a mixed group of workers, some of whom are employees and some aren't— people whom the manager may never see together as a group. Or a company that has developed ways of bringing workers up to speed fast on new Internet-based linking systems. Or a firm that helps supervisors see the benefits of diversity—à la the example in Chapter 8. You are a micro-company with a valuable product, and the expertise and knowledge to create extensions and spinoffs from that product.

Sometimes the overt business you are in is a cover or a front for the covert business you are in. Wal-Mart looks like a retail store, but it is actually in the business of moving merchandise in the most efficient way from its source to its user. Nordstrom appears to be a department store, but it is actually in the business of making people feel cared about. In the same sense, Mrs. Field's Cookies is actually in the business of making people happy. Southwest Airlines is actually in the business of making people forget what a hassle travel is and, hence, travel more. Charles Schwab is actually in the business of taking the confusion and frustration out of managing your own money. Boston Market Co. is actually in the business of making it less difficult and frustrating to be a two-career or a single-parent family.

Each of these businesses is also selling cookies or airline tickets or stocks and bonds or prepared food, of course. That's their overt business. But the covert business is the one that drives the important decisions and shapes the organization's culture. It is also the covert business that shapes the communication between the company and its market. And it is the success of the covert business that determines whether the organization prospers or not.

Sometimes an organization highlights its covert business to the point where it becomes overt. Andover Controls, a Massachusetts manufacturer of climate controls, began by emphasizing that business category. They sold to the construction market through electrical contractors, and it was difficult in that business to build a very strong product identity. Over time the company remedied that difficulty by shifting its focus toward "intelligent" buildings (where climate is integrated into a computer system that also takes care of security and utilities) and spotlighting its covert business. Andover Controls now says that it is "in the comfort business."

The Ritz-Carlton hotel chain is in the hotel business (overtly), but its covert business shows up in its motto, which every employee carries on a little card full of cues, maxims, reminders, and rules. The motto reads, "We are Ladies and Gentlemen serving Ladies and Gentlemen." They are covertly in the business of providing you with a personal staff when you are traveling. Organizational mottoes are usually tip-offs to the business that an organization is *really* in. If they aren't—if they simply are cute statements about the organization's overt business—they do not accomplish their goal.

Another clue to the real business that an organization is in is the narrative account that its people give about what they are, how they came to be, and why they are different from other, similar organizations. Every company has such a "story line," although you may have to infer it from employee interviews and an interpretive reading of company publications. Sometimes, however, an organization will be quite overt about its story line. Such is the case with Salon, a San Francisco–based publisher of a magazine on the Internet. Salon president David Zweig summarized the organization's story line in this way:

> *We are a tribe of journalists that has broken away from the pack. [We believe that] there is an appalling lack of quality on the Internet [and that] San Francisco is the creative epicenter of Internet content, the way Hollywood was for entertainment back in the teens. We have gathered up the brightest and happiest talent that was trapped in an aging technology and bureaucracy, that was oppressed by deadlines and space limitations.*

You ought to think about the "story" of your little You & Co. In fact, you probably already allude to the story in comments you make about what you do and why you do it. But making the story more conscious and coherent can help you to define your real business more clearly.

HOW TO REMODEL YOUR CAREER INTO A BUSINESS

Here, the first step is the big one: begin to think of everything you do as though it were being done by You & Co., not you individually. Let that basic idea begin to spread though your concerns and activities, asking yourself, "How would I think about this if 'I' were an organization, not an individual?" Start to differentiate the various organizational functions that your microbusiness needs to carry out. Play with the idea of "wearing many hats," as a way of thinking about them:

- The Marketing Hat
- The Product Development Hat
- The Operations Hat
- The Customer Service Hat
- The Sales Hat

- The Information Management Hat
- The Time Management Hat
- The Planning Hat

Your little microbusiness can't afford to play the big company game and hire specialists for each of these functions. Instead, you must combine your own efforts with those of external specialists who may be able to help you as consultants, temps, contractors, coventurers, or suppliers.

As you shift your thinking and action from an employee's perspective to a vendor mindset, you will need to go back through your list of hats again and again. You will make a decision, say, about marketing that has implications for your information management, and the decision you make in that area opens up customer service possibilities, which in turn changes the direction of your product development efforts; and each of these changes redefines the issues and possibilities in your day-to-day operations. So don't read too much into the sequence or segmentation of the following comments. I list them separately only because this book is sequential and analytical.

THE MARKETING HAT

As Chapter 7 made clear, the movement of work away from jobs has turned everyone into a marketer. Instead of working for an employer, we are each working for one or more clients. Instead of doing our job, we are helping the clients accomplish whatever it is that they are trying to accomplish. And instead of doing whatever our job descriptions prescribe and hoping that our activity meets the organization's need, we must study the markets that are available to us for clients who need services like ours and then sell our product to them. These necessities place responsibilities on us that we never had when we "had jobs."

When I was a college literature teacher (from 1961 to 1974), I arrived in my assigned classroom every September and found it full of students. What I was going to talk to them about was more or less set by the course description that had appeared in their catalogues—in my case, some area of American Literature or that time-honored course, Freshman English.

It never occurred to me to worry about how the students got there or whether they would, in fact, arrive. I actually did know something about how they got to the college, since my first college job had been in the field of admissions. But having left that job, I left behind any concern for the question of procurement. Nor did I give much thought to what the students were looking for when they arrived in my class. I spelled out very carefully what the class was and what it required just so that I would not have to deal with their misguided expectations. Having done those perfunctory bits of product description ("A survey of American literature, from the founding of the colonies to the Civil War . . ."), I settled back to do my job.

When I left teaching and started my personal learning and self-development business (although I never called it that), I was amazingly naive. I didn't think about the marketing I'd have to do. I just imagined that if I put out an interesting enough program description (a latter-day counterpart to my old course descriptions), the room would fill just as it had when I was a teacher.

Well, well, well. It didn't. I thought that what I had to do was publicize my seminars, but what I had to do was to learn all about my market and, specifically, why adults might want to pay money for something that would help them deal with the changes in their lives and their careers. I had to learn about their unmet needs, particularly the unmet needs that they didn't yet know how to describe. (Remember what we said in Chapter 8 about how difficult it is to educate your market. I ended up doing that, but it delayed my success for long and precious months.)

I have changed my product and my client group several times since those innocent days in the 1970s, and each time I have learned a little more about marketing. In the beginning, I had it all mixed up with sales, so that I was telling clients about the product when I should have been listening to what they were telling me they needed. I didn't even do the sales effectively, concentrating in teacherly fashion on why they ought to want what I had to offer instead of on how it would benefit them in some value-based way.

Since those days I've also learned to distinguish clients from customers. In the beginning it was easy, because the two groups were the same: the *customer* (the one who is the end-user and final beneficiary of what I was offering) and the *client* (the one who pays for the product and sets the terms for its delivery) were the same person. But as I moved into working with organizational clients, the customer-client bond came unstuck. The people who paid me were not the same people as the ones who sat in my seminars. Sometimes I got a little confused about whom I was serving.

As is so often the case, there's a short answer and a long answer to the dilemma raised by having clients who are not the same people as your customers. The short answer is, "Never promise the client that you will accomplish something that the customer hasn't agreed to." The longer answer begins by noting that customers seldom pay you directly, may not have the wherewithal to do so, and may not even know that you exist. So you'll need to market your product to your clients in terms of their ultimate success in serving their customers.

He who pays the piper gets to call the tune, but if no one dances (or marches, depending on your product) to the tune, the payer isn't well served and is likely to give up. So both the client and the customer are important, and there is no simple solution. You'll usually be in the business of helping clients accomplish what they want to vis-à-vis their customer. But sometimes you'll find that you can't retain your integrity unless you serve the customer more than the client intended you to.

I sometimes used to run into this problem when I was consulting with a client on some change that he or she was trying to bring about in an organization. The deeper I became involved in the situation, the more I realized that the change was going to make life harder for the people. "Just show me how to get the people to go along with it," the client would say. But I couldn't do what the client really wanted (i.e., make the people change). I had to find out how the change could be implemented in some way that would actually benefit the people—serve them, as it were. If I could do that, I could serve the client. But the client was sometimes unable to appreciate that, so I'd have to work unobtrusively.

Serving clients well is a tricky business, and reducing it to a rule is even harder. But beneath all the paradoxes is a simple truth. You need to provide what the market is seeking, and if it isn't seeking whatever you're providing, you have only three choices: to educate your clients (or customers), to look for a new market, or to develop a product that does meet the needs that your clients are experiencing.

I see all of my old misunderstandings and bad habits repeated today by most dejobbed workers. Whether they are still working as employees or have left their old employer and now work as independent workers, people are still imagining that if they "do a good job," You & Co. will operate smoothly. It is a variation on the *Field of Dreams* theme: "If you do your job, they will come!" Well, don't count on it.

Maybe you'd better go back and reread Chapter 7, "Finding Your Opportunity." You may even want to get some help in this matter, but we'll come to that later in this chapter. For now, recognize that you're going to have to wear your marketing hat a good deal of the time. If the prospect of doing this kind of marketing as well as delivering your product (not "doing your job") feels daunting to you, dust off your time management hat (see page 149).

THE PRODUCT DEVELOPMENT HAT

We spent Chapter 8 on "creating your product," so the short version of this subject is to say that you have to return to that issue (and maybe reread the chapter) fairly regularly. But there is more to the subject than that. In the first place, products have a natural life cycle. They may still do what they are supposed to do, but a whole new generation of competitors has appeared. Next to their offerings, your product looks like yesterday's news and last year's model.

And it isn't just that you will be upstaged by a competitor or that the market changes. Your D.A.T.A. and its interface with market needs can suggest many products. Or one product suggests another version of the same thing—product extensions, they call them in the business. Or your product is very cyclical—lots of demand and then little—and you wish you could diversify into some other products that would zig when your first one zags. One way or another, that original product—good as we all hope it will prove—isn't the annuity that you'll be able to retire on.

You can learn a lot about product development by reading about how big businesses do it. Look for articles on 3M and Hewlett-Packard especially, because they are awfully good at it. And learn from the failures too, as when a company is sure that the market is calling for something new (remember New Coke?) or when a company diversifies so much that it loses its identity in its customers' eyes (can you even recall what Primerica does?). Notice how some products don't have a market until they actually exist, because people don't understand them as concepts: the computer mouse is just one example.

However you handle it, product development is going to be an ongoing part of your little business. On the one hand, product development is a subset of marketing, for as you talk to your clients and (whenever possible) to their customers, you need to keep your eyes and ears open for emerging and perhaps not-yet-well-defined needs. I didn't say it back in Chapter 8, but creating a product is an open-ended task. Change creates new unmet needs; other providers satisfy your clients better than you do; and you yourself change—in your desires and assets, at least, and certainly in your understanding of what the jobshift is and how to deal with it. So product development cannot cease.

THE OPERATIONS HAT

One of my first big clients was a manufacturing company, and my main customer there was its executive group. Around the table were hotshot executives from Design, Marketing, Sales, Testing, Human Resources, and the product groups. Along with them sat a big, heavy-browed, slow-moving vice president of operations. The rest of the group treated him the way a family might treat the cousin who was decidedly slow but who had inherited all the money. They couldn't do without the guy. All the company's products came out of his shop. Without him there'd be no profits. He wasn't swift, but he was essential.

Well, it may be like that in You & Co. too. Those everyday tasks—returning calls, getting the copying machine fixed, sending out the mailing on time, checking the invoices, keeping track of credit card balances—aren't sexy or even very interesting to most people. But if they're not done right, your goose is microwaved. The operations hat is not glamorous, although for people of some temperaments it involves the satisfying activity of getting things shipshape. But whatever your temperament, operations is so important that it needs to be on your regular to-do list.

THE CUSTOMER SERVICE HAT

How are you doing with your client? Does your product help the client's customer? How do you know?

Are you checking regularly with your clients and their customers on how you're doing? Do you have an easy and effective way to find out how you're doing? Do you thank your clients for telling you how you're doing? Do you make the small, quick changes in what you're doing that show more powerfully than words can that you care what your clients think? Do you have product documentation and client-education materials to increase the value that people receive from what you provide?

These are the questions that matter when you are wearing the customer service hat. When I was a teacher, I was amazed at how uninterested most of my fellow teachers were in whether their services were effective or in how they could improve what they did. I have to admit that I myself took negative feedback fairly badly, chalking it up to the lack of interest and aptitude in my students as often as I blamed it on what I had or hadn't done. But I *did* hold office hours, during which we pored over a past class or a past paper to make sure that the student understood what was expected and how to get better results the next time. Not very sophisticated "customer service," but better than nothing.

Of course, I wasn't really in competition with other teachers because I had tenure. I worked very hard. But it never occurred to me that the college could outsource my course next semester or bring in a temp to teach it. We were evaluated, of course. Job holders usually are. But what counted in the evaluation was a lot of other things (the papers I published, the committees I served on, the enrollment in my courses, the public lectures I gave) and not how I served the customer. "Customer service" was not an educational concept, and so the lack of it never threatened my job. Well, the lack of customer service will certainly threaten You & Co.

No matter what you do and how secure your position seems to be, you are in direct competition with more people than you imagine. Add to that the fact that customers have learned over the past decade or two to demand good customer service and to go elsewhere if they don't get it, and you get a situation in which you must make sure that clients and customers not only *get* good service but also *experience* how they are treated as excellent service.

THE SALES HAT

All of these hats were jobs in the old world of integrated companies. Sales was the job of salespeople. It was a job that involved talking a customer into buying. That was an essentially adversarial process, because the customer didn't want to buy. That was a given. It was the salesperson's job to break down that resistance and close the deal.

Sales was both a function and a skill. If you had the skill, you could sell anything because you "knew how to sell." The salesman (and they usually were men) had his own little tap-dance routine that he claimed always worked. If you couldn't see yourself doing those dumb things and telling those corny jokes, well then, sales probably wasn't for you! That attitude is not dead, but it doesn't work very well in a dejobbed world, and the rewards for successful selling are no longer going to those who view sales that way.

In a dejobbed world, sales is an offshoot of marketing. It involves understanding exactly what the client's unmet needs are and how one's product would or wouldn't meet them. This selling is collaborative, and a sale that does not meet a real need is not a sale that is worth making. Every sale that *does* meet such a need leaves the kind of highly satisfied client that is the whole purpose of the business. Satisfied clients keep coming back.

This is not a text on selling, so my point here is not to instruct you in how to do it. Instead, I want to frame selling in the present context as helping clients understand your product and its benefits and helping them to choose how best to get their needs met. I also want to remind you that sales feeds back into product development by showing how the present product fails to meet the need, as well as how it—or something else— could be better.

In talking about dejobbing to many audiences, I've found that one of the commonest worries of present job holders is that in this new workplace (and the workers' new roles as microbusinesses), "You'd have to be selling all the time, and I'm just not a salesperson." There are a couple of related misunderstandings here, and victims of them are at a great disadvantage.

First, the idea of *selling* is skewed. This isn't fast talk and the song-and-dance stuff that we grew up imagining sales to be. This selling is talking about a product that is aligned with your own D.A.T.A, so you believe in it. This selling is based on a real understanding of and sympathy with the customer's unmet need, so it isn't putting anything over on anyone. And the idea that you can't talk about what you believe in and what the client needs simply doesn't withstand the test of experience. We can all "sell" under those circumstances.

Second, the idea that such selling takes too much time and distracts you from your real task of doing or making belongs back in the old job world. In that world, selling was a full-time job, and if you had another full-time job you couldn't sell too. But in the dejobbed world, these functions overlap with one another. As one delivers the product, one is alert to customer service issues and listens with a marketer's ear, generating input into the product design process. Selling is just this whole complex of activities when they bump into a prospective customer. They are mutually supportive, and none of them is your "job." To say, "Here's an idea; it worked well for one of my other clients" is easy and a natural part of the interaction with a client. Selling doesn't take some unusual kind of talent.

THE INFORMATION MANAGEMENT HAT

There are scarcely any business activities today that have not been affected by information technology (IT). Many of them have been transformed. Easily accessible and analyzable data about clients and projects are as critical to the success of You & Co. as they are to a big business. In fact, one of the gifts of the IT revolution is that it has put small firms (including one-person "businesses") on a footing that is surprisingly comparable to that occupied by big firms. The little outfit's proposal can be as attractive, the data as convincing, and the billing as quick and as accurate as those of the big outfit. They can be even better, in fact, since they don't have to be approved by all those job holders who are fighting over turf issues.

But this potentiality has to be realized for You & Co. to thrive. For many dejobbed workers, the expertise necessary to accomplish the task is best gained with outside help, but there is an advantage in going through a time when you can't afford to pay for it. For doing everything yourself is the best course you can take in what actually needs to be done. So view the first couple of years, when you are making mistakes and doing things for which you have no talent, as a training program specially designed for you.

The information management hat is what you put on anytime you think about whatever you know about your clients and how you could learn more. Are you keeping track of the right information about them? Do you have a way to schedule and track the work you do for them? How can you use what you know about them to segment your potential clients into categories that are easier to understand as slightly different markets? How can you organize all of this information into a database that you can use most easily?

The old box of file cards, the handwritten client lists, and the folders in the filing cabinet become outdated pretty quickly these days. If the prospect of using a computer to store and organize this information makes you hyperventilate, you'd better get some training or some help. You are going to need the hardware, the software, and the knowledge to make all of this mixing and sorting of information possible.

Like the other hats, however, information management isn't "a job" the way it was in the old-style organization. Instead, it's one of the overlapping circles that we keep talking about, circles that cluster around the marketing hat. Information management is just the way you manage what you know about your market and how you communicate with your market. If your product is a knowledge-based product, as it is increasingly likely to be, information management is also a way to develop your product in all its client-ready variations.

Learning about information management is like learning a foreign language. It's relatively hard to do if it is just a subject you study, a subject with little relation to what you really want to accomplish. But if you are motivated by real desire, it is different. Imagine that you've just fallen in love—totally head over heels in love—with someone in Japan. It's amazing how quickly you'd start picking up Japanese phrases, isn't it? The moral to that fable is to keep your eye on what it is that you want to accomplish, and to keep your learning projects closely tied to those goals. When "learning what you need to know" becomes "a subject," the same thing happens that happens when "doing whatever needs to be done" becomes "a job." Motivation falls, efficiency declines, and it's no longer fun to come to work.

THE TIME MANAGEMENT HAT

I feel strange writing briefly about things that others write books about and devote careers to. My intent, in all of these matters, is not to give you a minicourse in the subject but to show how the subject is relevant and what issues you particularly need to attend to if you are to operate successfully outside the perimeters of a traditional job. Time management clearly belongs on the list of things you need to be good at.

One of the benefits of a job is that it has boundaries and a core of responsibility. The boundaries tell you that *that stuff* is his job, not yours, so you don't have to worry about it. They also tell you when it is time to go home at night, even though the report isn't finished. The core of job responsibility gives you a spool to wind your activities around and a basis on which to calculate priorities. When you give up being job-centered, you lose those reference points. Everything crowds in on you, demanding your attention. You may find yourself with multiple projects and multiple clients. You start to realize that regular hours were an artifact of the job world and that voice mail, faxes, and e-mail have delivered the final coup de grace to them. Everything you have to do—everything you could do—is waiting for you in the little laptop in your briefcase, so your work is always with you now.

How do you get everything done? Wrong question! How do you get the most important things done? Right question. How do you figure out which things are important, how do you lay out your day, and how do you give some of your overflowing to-do list to others? Good questions.

As I say, my purpose is not to write another treatise on time management but simply to say that if you are not good at managing your time, then you'd better get good at it. Find a book you like at the nearest bookstore, ask your stationery store for suggestions about materials, and check with your local community college for a course to help you do that. More people fail as dejobbed workers because they don't have the self-management skills than fail because they lack a good education or the right kind of experience.

This is not a new challenge, however. Every time the conditions of work change in any significant way, the way in which people deal with time changes too. In the pre-industrial world, clock time hardly existed. Although the hours might be struck on the church or town hall clock, most people lived by the laws of light and dark, warmth and cold. Their tasks had a rhythm that alternated between periods in which there was a huge amount to be done—a crop to be harvested, for example—and periods in which little could be done because of darkness or bad weather.

Industrialism flattened out the rhythm into an even stream of activity, then punctuated that with bells and whistles to signal times of starting and stopping. Wealthy men began to carry pocket watches, and they gained the power to make people hurry and worry when they took the watches out, frowned, and announced that it was nearly six o'clock. The railroads required standardized time zones.

People began by finding clock time an alien idea and hating it. It was mechanical, they said, and inhuman. But like many great innovations, clock time started as something that people thought that they'd never be able to live with and ended as something that people said they couldn't live without. As it was developed into regular hours, different shifts, workdays, weekends, and all the other time boundaries that gave shape to people's lives, clock time became familiar and even almost friendly.

But now it's wild again. The new night shift, says a recent article on work, is the all-night work sessions that people at go-go companies are expected to put in as deadlines approach. People talk seriously about whether they should take their pager along on vacation. Articles on insomnia suggest that you shouldn't just lie there counting the hours; you should get up and do something. (Your laptop is downstairs in your briefcase.) Cellular phones are sold as ways to make your commute productive. Time on the stationary bicycle is used to catch up on the news, and time jogging in the park is tapped for self-improvement via a tape-recorded version of a book digest (whole books are needlessly long).

As in so many other ways, we're in a transitional period as far as time is concerned. We don't have the new habits yet to help us to deal automatically with the new conditions of our lives. It takes a couple of generations to get those. And in the meantime, we'll need to turn to books and courses and coaches and leather-covered planners to help us. (Hey, do you suppose there is a *condensed* version of the time management book that I could read when I jog tomorrow morning? Twenty minutes would be about right.)

THE PLANNING HAT

Companies have planning departments, which means that they have turned planning into a job. It also means that planning is no longer the natural by-product of marketing and product development and that it becomes something that there is never time enough left in the day to get to. In You & Co., planning must be an everyday affair in which you ask, "What am I going to have to do to get where I want to go?" And also, occasionally, "And where is it that I really want to go?"

You first need to make a plan for launching You & Co., and we will go over the way to do that in the next chapter. What we want to cover here is the ongoing planning process and the issues that are going to keep coming up as you do it. This is not planning with a capital *P*, which you do when you write a strategic plan to persuade a banker to lend you start-up money. The chances are that if You & Co. needs start-up money beyond living expenses for a few months and the initial purchase of your basic equipment, you've got yourself turned around and are starting up an old-fashioned small business, not a You & Co.

The planning you need to do will produce to-do lists but not vinyl-covered "planning documents." It's meant for you, not your banker. It tells you where you're going and how to get there; it isn't a piece of puffery intended to persuade someone to give you money. It is intended to provide you with the resources you need and the path you intend to follow. And because change is in the driver's seat in this whole dejobbed world, it provides you with Plan B if circumstances send Plan A into the shredder.

Here are some of the issues that you will want to cover in your planning. These are questions to raise each time you consider taking a new direction or doing a new thing, as well as whenever you are standing back to survey the territory that lies ahead. They are questions that are never settled once and for all, and they do not lead to some magic, comprehensive blueprint that is complete and needs only to be carried out. They are more like checklists that assure you that you haven't forgotten your lunch or your sunblock.

Here are those issues:

Skills and Knowledge

What are the skills or the knowledge that you need to run You & Co. effectively? And what do you need to fill in the gaps in your assets? If you are still working for an organization, the training may be close at hand. But even then you've got to arrange for it and spend the time to get it. I guess you need another hat for You & Co.: the training hat.

Benefits

Darn. Another hat! They are rare workers today who can be sure that retirement is comfortably provided for or that they have the money to pay for the health services they may need. And everyone acknowledges that "today's workers will have to take more responsibility" for those things. But no one ties that to the fact that the carrier of those benefits, the job, is disappearing from the scene. Needless to say, I want you to go beyond taking "more responsibility" for your financial security. It needs to be part of the long-term planning for You & Co.

Space and Equipment

Where are you going to work? The job gave a ready-made answer to that question, but dejobbing forces you to make up your own answer. Even if you have a cubicle or a station on the factory floor, you also need the space and equipment to work at home, and you may need the equipment to work wherever else you spend time—in a hotel, at a client location, or in transit.

Cards and Brochures

If you leave the job world entirely, these things will be important to communicate who you are and what you do. If you stay in the job world but run You & Co. as a covert operation, these things can still be important. What does your business card say that you are? (Well, your *imaginary* business card, then.) And putting together a brochure for You & Co., even if you'll never give an actual copy of it to a client, can be a wonderful way of focusing your awareness of what your product is and why a client should pay for it.

Time

We've already talked about time planning, but this is just a reminder that time is a resource that you are going to need to set aside to launch You & Co. It may be time spent on a course or time spent putting together a simple "brochure." It may be time spent at professional meetings where you can strengthen your network, or it may be time spent reading a book.

Money

As I have already said, most new-style small businesses don't require the loans and lines of credit that yesterday's small businesses did. But if you're leaving the job world, you'll still need living expenses. And if you decide that you need a fax machine to launch You & Co., you'll have that kind of start-up cost too. There may be lean times, as there were when all three of my own first consulting clients decided to terminate our projects at the same time. But big investments and borrowing to meet payrolls is not what You & Co. is about. And if your expenses start to get out of hand, head back to square one.

Structure

It sounds funny to talk about the "structure" of You & Co., for it is mostly just you and you and all those darned hats. But remember that you are part of a networked economy and that even the smallest company (*especially* a very small company) has to outsource a lot of what it does. Here are some structural supports to consider:

- Suppliers and Support Services. Just as the auto companies outsource the manufacture of over half of the parts in your car, you are going to have to find some good suppliers of the products and services you need regularly. While it is fine to shop around, your goal is to get regular suppliers and educate them about your needs and capabilities so that you can count on them as though they were coworkers in the office down the hall.
- Joint Venturers. Because you are small and focused on your particular product(s), it makes sense to tackle larger projects in the company of others and even to clump together informally to do so. It also makes sense to find other firms that specialize in helping you to leverage what you do individually. Such firms are springing up in response to the unbundling that is going on today, firms like Venture Initiatives, a company that markets and distributes products based on the work of independent inventors.

■ Consultants. People joke about consultants being people who are between jobs, but the reality is that an enormous amount of work that
used to be done and advice that used to be given by full-time resident
experts can be done and given more effectively by people who come
in for that project and then leave. The people who simply hang out
the consultant shingle while they wait for a job offer are far less significant than the people who see the handwriting on the wall and
turn their D.A.T.A. into a consulting business. Their market is being
created by the same forces that sent them out on their own too.

■ Coaching. While consultants have been around for a long time,
"coaches" haven't, and nothing so clearly points to the coming of age
of the freelance worker as the appearance of the coach, a person who
serves as an adviser for pay to independent workers who are trying to
hone the skills they need to run their You & Co.'s. There is even a
Coach University now, conducting on-line training from a base in
Salt Lake City. Its enrollment has tripled in the past year and now
stands at 350.

■ "Board of Directors" for You & Co. The final structural element you
may want to consider is an informal "board" for your little company.
Here the advice is collective and offered on a volunteer basis by people who enjoy the experience of getting to know each other and
working together on a project.

FINALLY, YOUR CAREER PATH OPTIONS

I keep reminding you that this book's advice will help you to cope with the
forces of dejobbing, whether you plan to stay in your present job or head
off on your own. But that way of saying it considerably oversimplifies the
options that you actually have before you. Here are all the different set-
tings in which you might choose to run You & Co.:

1. Look for the unmet needs and the work that needs doing in the big,
   public market or in your community, and launch an actual little
   start-up company to do it. Most of the You & Co. ideas would be useful even if you hope your little company will grow and, if fate allows,
   become a big company. You're following the time-honored entrepreneurial route here.

2. Look for the unmet needs and the work that needs doing in your industry or your profession and launch an actual little start-up company to do it. The same hopes would apply, and you'll be following the same route. Remember not to let your growing company get job-bound, though.

3. Look for the unmet needs of your present organizational employer (or a past one) and launch your start-up company to meet them. Same advice as number 2.

4. Look for the unmet needs of your present organizational employer and go to work for a consultancy or a contractor who will view your experience and contacts with your firm as assets that make you valuable enough to hire. Make sure that you are not just trading a job for a job—even a better one. Make sure that the new setting helps you to avoid some of the traps of the job world.

5. Look for the unmet needs of your present organizational employer and propose that you leave your present job and take them on as a special project. Here, You & Co. would function like a little in-house consultant or contractor. This might give you the flexibility of the new order without giving up the security of the old order. It *might*. With time, it is more likely that you and the company would part ways. (If this happens, in the exit interview they'll tell you that you're not the loyal worker you used to be. What they won't bother to acknowledge is that you have actually outlasted several thousand "loyal" workers who were cut in the last rounds of downsizing.)

6. Look for the unmet needs of your present organization and seek out another job there that better positions you to meet those needs and build security by being valuable to the organization. This tactic involves trying to pour the new wine (You & Co.) into an old bottle (a job). In an enlightened company, it could be a good option; otherwise, it is probably a temporary solution. Still, it may be a good option to try while you plan your next move.

7. Remodel your present job so that it is more in tune with the realities of a workplace that is rapidly being dejobbed. Get out in front of these changes. Same comments as above, with the qualification that

your present job isn't as likely to be one that you can reorient toward unmet needs as one chosen specifically for that quality would be.

8. Hang on, don't make eye contact with anyone, and hope that all of this "dejobbing" stuff blows over. What can I say? I hope that you are really, really close to retirement, because the life expectancy of this solution is really, really short.

In the next chapter you'll be putting together your own personal plan, so the real application of these ideas comes then. For now, the best thing you can do is review the main points covered in this chapter and decide how they best fit into your own situation, resources, and product possibilities.

THE STRENGTHS OF YOU & CO.

Step One

Name one way in which, in your everyday work activities, you currently operate as though the decisions you make are based on building up a tiny one-person business, not just doing (or looking for) a job. Then look for other ways to incorporate the You & Co. mentality into your daily work.

_____

Step Two

State what business You & Co. is in. Remember that this won't be the business that your employer is in. It's *your* business.

_____

Step Three

Distinguish You & Co.'s overt business—your conventional business category—from the covert or real business—what you're doing for your client.

Overt   Covert

_____   _____

Step Four

Write a motto that captures the essence of the real business you run.

_____

Step Five

Sketch out the "story line" for You & Co., a distinctive account of what you are and do, how you came to do it, and why your version of "it" is what a client really needs.

_____

_____

_____

_____

_____

_____

Step Six

On a scale of 1 to 10 (with 10 being the best) rate your current performance under each of these hats:

1. The Marketing Hat _____
2. The Product Development Hat _____
3. The Operations Hat _____
4. The Customer Service Hat _____
5. The Sales Hat _____
6. The Information Management Hat _____
7. The Time Management Hat _____
8. The Planning Hat _____

On the same scale of 1 to 10, rate You & Co. on the quality of the following resources available to it:

9. Skills and Knowledge   _____

10. Benefits Program   _____

11. Space and Equipment   _____

12. Cards and Brochures   _____

13. Time and Schedule   _____

14. Structure and Help   _____

15. Suppliers and Services   _____

16. Joint Venturers   _____

17. Consultants   _____

18. Coaching   _____

19. "Board of Directors"   _____

Step Seven

Add up the numerical scores you assigned to yourself on the nineteen questions above. How'd you do? Don't be discouraged if your total was in the 30s or 40s or 50s. Why wouldn't it be, after all those years of being taught and told to "do your job"?

Use your score to identify where you should work to improve You & Co.'s chance for success. Remember that 7 out of 10 is a C–, which is barely acceptable in the grade world. To position yourself to capitalize on dejobbing, you need to score between 8 and 9. Top performers will, of course, score higher.

A low score is just the alarm clock's ring: Time to Wake Up! The next chapter will help you to stop evaluating and start acting.

CHAPTER TEN

Making Your Plan and Getting Started

It had long since come to my attention that people of accomplishment rarely sat back and let things happen to them. They went out and happened to things.

—Elinor Smith

Every one must row with the oars he has.

—English proverb

BUSINESS PLANS

Most business plans are useless for the task ahead of you because they are really rationales for someone to lend you money. You need a plan that helps you to focus your energies and to be sure that each thing you do is actually forwarding the development of You & Co. So what follows is a description of the steps or stages of your undertaking.

Read them reflectively and then set them aside for a few days. When you pick them up again, go to the point in the progression where you think you are. Read over that step a couple of times; then set the book aside and use what you have read as a springboard for your own thinking. If you can do this reading with someone else and do the thinking as give-and-take, so much the better. If you can't involve someone else, get a piece of paper and write out your thinking.

If you do that, write quickly and without too much forethought—the way you'd say it if you were speaking. Don't worry if you interject ideas that pop into your head as you write or if the sequence of the ideas is jumbled. Don't worry if you aren't quite translating your ideas into coherent prose. Just keep writing. The purpose is to capture the possibilities that are going round and round in your head. You can select, prune, refine, and polish them later. For now, read . . . think . . . and write or talk.

Start with wherever you are in the developmental sequence. Go back occasionally to pick up loose threads in not-quite-complete (or I'd-better-take-another-shot-at-that-one) steps. Take time to do the planning and investigating and acting upon one step before you go on in any serious way to deal with the next step. This isn't something to read through and then put aside as finished. This final chapter is short, but it should take you much longer to get through than the rest of the book combined.

That's all. The pretrip lecture is finished. Pack up your stuff and hit the road. Rest when you're tired, but then pick up your stuff and get going again. And remember why you're on this path: because the old roads are washing out in the vocational storm of the century. You're heading for the economic high ground. There are a number of others there already and they'll show you what to do when you get there. Bon voyage. Maybe our paths will cross. I hope so.

STAGE ONE

Decide what business you are in. If you aren't ready to do that, reread Chapters 3–6 on your resources and Chapter 7 on your markets to get a better grip on your product. That should help your business come more clearly into focus. Say, I forgot to ask: if your business had a name, what would it be? See, there; *that's* the business you're in! Keep coming back to the mantra of *I'm in the business of. . . . I'm in the business of. . . . I'm in the business of. . . .* It will help you at all those unmarked crossroads you're going to encounter.

STAGE TWO

What is your product? Yes, I know you answered that back in Stage One as a way to point you toward your business. But you didn't *really* answer it. What, exactly, is it that you are selling?

- Is it really a reflection of what you Desire at this point in your life?
- Does it really make the best use of your Abilities?
- Does it really fit and benefit from your Temperament?
- Does it really draw upon your Assets?
- And does it really answer some unmet need in the market you have chosen to serve?

If you are unsure about any of these matters, Chapters 3–7 should be a help, and Chapter 8 is about integrating D.A.T.A. and market need into a product. Any of these matters is something that may need more work. Talk them over with someone whose judgment you trust. Go for outside help—to a career or psychological counselor—if you can't make sense out of your own responses. But do keep your own independent viewpoint intact, because the chances are that they are in the I-help-people-to-find-jobs business. Do whatever you need to do to understand your D.A.T.A. and your market possibilities. And then build them into your product.

STAGE THREE

Who is this client of yours? (Again, I know you have already answered that. We're going in at a deeper level this time.) Who is this client and what does he or she need? To understand the need, consider the client's customer. What does the client need to satisfy the customer? What is the customer looking for, and how could you help the client to satisfy the customer more completely? Do you need more information to answer these questions? Go out and get it. Do you need advice or help? Ditto.

STAGE FOUR

This is all fine, but if the client can't see the need or can't imagine you as the solution, it's all just words. Can you make a case for this client coming to you to get this need met? How will what you have to offer solve the problem or exploit the possibility? How is it better than other ways to do those things? Why should the client listen to you? What's your story, anyway? (What is *your story*? You & Co. probably existed long before you read this book. You just have to reframe your career as a business story.) What resources do you need to make your case believable?

STAGE FIVE

And what do you need to develop You & Co. into the microbusiness that clients turn to when they have needs like the one(s) you are set up to satisfy? At first, you'll just be trying to get the ball back over the net, but as time goes on you'll find yourself wanting to develop your organization further. Remember the hats.

- The Marketing Hat
- The Product Development Hat
- The Operations Hat
- The Customer Service Hat
- The Sales Hat
- The Information Management Hat
- The Time Management Hat
- The Planning Hat

It'll take juggling to keep them all airborne, but juggling gets easier as you do it. Treat your setbacks as lessons and keep moving.

STAGE SIX

There's a whole spectrum of possibilities out there, everything from trying to change-proof your job to striking out on your own as an entrepreneur. But those are just external differences—big differences, to be sure, but just external. Inwardly, they share a mindset: *You're nobody's hired hand. You're an independent business, a business with clients.* OK. What kind of business development do you need?

STEP SEVEN

Although this may have been clear from all that we said about how important honoring your temperament is, let's make it explicit: there is no one path to the goal you are seeking. When British Telecom did a study of the people who started their own businesses—because, very wisely, they wanted to encourage those qualities in their employees—they found not one pattern but four:

- Some people were *networkers,* who parlayed their contacts and friendships into "opportunities" that they then exploited.
- Others were *past masters,* who were very, very good at something and built a product of such quality that clients sought it out.
- Still others were *charmers,* who talked their way through to clients and persuaded them on the merits of argument and the power of their style.
- Finally, others were *hunters,* who knew everything about their clients and all the strategies that they'd need to catch them.

Are these different abilities or different temperaments? Are they based on different desires or different assets? The answer is *yes, all of the above.* But whichever is your own natural path, follow it. All the paths lead to the summit.

CONCLUSION

You're going to be making it up as you go along from here on. I'm aware of the irony of giving advice about that process, because if the advice could really be followed you wouldn't have to make it up. It would exist already. Like those jobs that we grew up believing were *out there,* waiting for us. They're not gone, those jobs, but they are going. And many of those that remain are miserably paid or being given to temps.

But there's still *work* out there waiting to be done, needing to be done, not yet boxed up into *jobs.* There are no ads for it, nor are there postings on the board outside the Personnel (or "Placement") Office. It isn't even an *opening* yet. Just sombeody's annoyance or worry or suspicion or frustration or hope or wish or idea or dream. Those are the things you'll want to look for, not jobs. What are you waiting for?

Afterword

I never finish a book without being tormented by an awareness of all that I didn't say. I suspect that the art of writing is made up largely of knowing how to start and when to stop, and that succumbing to the temptation not to stop has ruined many an otherwise good book.

But in this case I am troubled by the fact that in aiming this book at individuals, I leave the impression that this is just an individual issue. In fact the disappearance of jobs is a huge societal issue—perhaps the largest issue of our times, since it has left so many people confused and discouraged about how they can make a living. Confused, discouraged, and *angry*, because at bottom many of the incomprehensible acts of violence that fill the daily paper spring from an inarticulate sense that *they* changed the rules in the middle of the game.

The only workable solution to the issues raised by dejobbing would involve a new, integrated social initiative by five distinctly different parts of the social order.

1. Corporations and institutions, which face the task of transforming their workers from job holders into people who will do what needs to be done. Organizational training departments need to reorient their efforts toward this end.

2. Governments at every level, which face the double task of dismantling the old policies and services that fit a world in which people

had jobs but don't fit the dejobbed world; and creating new policies and services that fit a world in which jobs are no longer the norm.

3. Unions and professional associations, which have often seen their mission as one of ensuring job security but which must now be transformed by the demands of their own members into organizations that provide dejobbed workers with what they need: education and training, help with benefits, advice about self-managed careers, and a sense of community to replace "the company."

4. Schools and colleges, which have to reorient their offerings to a world in which people aren't going to get anything but the droppings if they lack basic educational skills, and in which people are going to have to continue to develop themselves throughout their careers.

5. And finally, new institutions and services, some of which will be for profit and some of which will be nonprofit. The whole field of career development and work search is full of unmet needs. It may be, for example, that today's sometimes hard-hearted temp agency contains the germ of a whole new social institution that would replace the corporation as the pathing mechanism for careers and the provider of benefits.

I mention these parts of our society because I ducked past them in the text of the book. Maybe that is my next book. But I mention them also because they are so full of unmet needs that many readers ought to be scanning them for markets as they search for ways to find work. Whenever there is a huge social change, opportunities don't just disappear in one place and turn up again in a new place. Many of the opportunities are created within the change process itself. You shouldn't overlook them.

The good news is that if you are reading this book, you are already ahead of the crowd. For at least another generation, people are going to be doing the old job-hunting thing. Like people who, when the key won't go in the lock, just jab it in again and again, they cannot see that they are operating on the wrong assumptions.

But who can blame them? Our press feeds those old assumptions with stories about "The 10 Best Jobs for the 21st Century." The government feeds those same assumptions by tracking the "job figures" as though they were the vital signs of a sick society. Companies feed those assumptions with all their out-of-date job descriptions and their job-based hiring. And colleges and social agencies feed those assumptions by setting up placement centers. *Placement,* for heaven's sake! As though there were these nice peg holes of various shapes out there, and we just had to match them up with the pegs!

We're entering a new age, folks, and we are going to be working out the implications of that fact for as long as we're around. Clearly, no final answer will be possible until we figure out how to get these five big institutional players (corporations, government, labor, education, and emerging institutions) around the table. But that is sure to take a while. So why don't you launch You & Co. while you're waiting?

Notes

Foreword

Page viii: "the decline-of-the-job thesis": *JobShift: How to Prosper in a Workplace Without Jobs* (Reading, Mass.: Addison-Wesley Publishing Co., 1994). If you are primarily interested in the evidence for dejobbing and an analysis of its organizational implications, I hope that you will start with *JobShift*.

Page xi: Thurman Arnold: Quoted in John W. Gardner and Francesca Gardner Reese, *Quotations of Wit and Wisdom* (New York: W. W. Norton, 1975), p. 196.

Chapter One

Page 5: Quoted in Jay Finegan, "Out but Not Down," *Inc.* [The *Inc. 500 1996* issue], p. 49. Dresner's company is run by three people who lost jobs at DEC, and was #10 on *Inc.*'s 1996 list of the five hundred fastest-growing small companies in America.

Page 6: Bank economists: Bernard Wysocki, Jr., "Seers in a Slump," *Wall Street Journal,* October 9, 1995, p. A1.

Page 6: Jon Tipping: See Clare Hogg, "The Angel of Business," *Enterprise* (U.K.), March–April, 1996, p. 55.

Page 7: Restoration Co.: Leslie Helms, "Workers Brave a New World," *Los Angeles Times,* December 10, 1995, p. D1.

Page 7: Lotus and Olsten Co.: Julie Cohen Mason, "A Temp-ting Staffing Strategy," *Management Review,* February, 1996, pp. 33–36.

Page 7: Alessandra Bianchi, "Breaking Away," *Inc.,* November, 1995, pp. 36–41. And Jeff Cole, "Boeing Teaches Employees How to Run Small Business, *Wall*

Street Journal, November 7, 1995, p. B1. Not only does Boeing's initiative provide future vendors who know the company well; it also, according to a state government official who helped start the program, "hold[s] down [Boeing's] unemployment insurance contributions and improve[s] its image in the community, [as well as fostering] . . . peace with unions by providing long-term employment for workers who are unlikely to be called back because of long-term cost-cutting programs." Ibid., p. B2.

Page 7: Electronic Scriptorium: See Jyoti Thottam, "Entrepreneur Finds Monks Make Heavenly Employees," *Wall Street Journal,* July 12, 1993.

Page 8: Reuters Holdings: "Signs of the Times," (n.a.), *Training & Development,* February, 1996, p. 33.

Page 9: "the real, controlling resource . . .": Peter Drucker, *Post-Capitalist Society* (New York: HarperCollins, 1993), p. 6.

Page 10: "Operating effectively . . .": Robert Howard, "The CEO as Organizational Architect: An Interview with Xerox's Paul Allaire," *Harvard Business Review,* September–October, 1992, p. 109.

Page 11: Cheryl Russell: See her article "The Master Trend" in *American Demographics,* October, 1993. The quotations cited here are from pages 30 ff.

Page 13: "Economic friction . . .": See "The Friction-Free Economy," by John Case, *Inc.,* June, 1996, pp. 27–28.

Page 15: Customer versus client: For more about distinguishing between a client and a customer, see page 142. Basically, the client is the user of your services and the customer is the user of the client's services. What you do for your clients will help them to serve their customers, and your services are only justified by the value you add to the clients' services to those customers.

Page 16: Robert Schaen: Quoted in Janice Castro, "Disposable Workers," *Time,* March 29, 1993, p. 47.

Page 16: For a very interesting study of the movie industry as the prototype for tomorrow's dejobbed industry, see Joel Kotkin, "Why Every Business Will Be Like Show Business," *Inc.,* March, 1995, pp. 64ff.

Page 17: "No one says, 'We'll help you'": Quoted in Tohas A. Stewart, "3M Fights Back," *Fortune,* February 5, 1996, p. 99.

Page 18: "You won't last at Microsoft . . .": Quoted in Bob Flipczak, "Beyond the Gates at Microsoft," *Training,* September, 1993, p. 43.

Page 18: "if people want to change": Ibid.

Page 18: Peter Schwartz quote: Robert McGarvey, "Tomorrow Land" [an interview with Schwartz and Stewart Brand], *Entrepreneur,* February, 1996, p. 138.

Page 21: Alfred North Whitehead: John W. Gardner and Francesca Gardner Reese, *Quotations of Wit and Wisdom* (New York: W. W. Norton, 1975), p. 195.

Page 21: Henry Thomas Buckle: George Seldes, *The Great Quotations* (Secaucus, N.J. The Citadel Press, 1983).

Chapter Two

Page 27: Lily Tomlin and Jane Wagner: Quoted in Robert Byrne, *The Fourth and by Far the Most Recent 637 Best Things Anybody Ever Said* (New York: Fawcett, 1990), #45.

Page 29: People who did not go beyond high school: Brigid McMenamin, "Whatever It Takes," *Forbes,* March 27, 1995, p. 134.

Page 29: Lewis Perelman: *School's Out* (New York: Avon Books, 1992).

Page 30: Henry Bessemer: Quoted in John W. Gardner and Francesca Gardner Reese, *Quotations of Wit and Wisdom* (New York: W. W. Norton, 1975), p. 18.

Page 31: Jackie Larson, "To Get a Job, Be a Pest," *Wall Street Journal,* April 14, 1995, p. A12.

Page 32: *Forbes FYI* assistant: Leah Garchik, "A Treasure Hunt Is Part of the Job Application," *San Francisco Chronicle,* January 26, 1996, p. D20.

Page 33: Jim McCann: Jenny C. McCune, "Flower Power," *Management Review,* March, 1995, p. 9.

Page 33: Ten Basic Skills: From "Research Capsules," *Training & Development,* December, 1995, p. 51.

Page 34: Samuel Metters: From *Inc. Technology,* 1995:3, p. 79.

Page 35: Nordstrom: The first quotation is from company spokesperson Vicki Woo and is quoted in *Bottom Line/Business,* July 1, 1995, p. 15; the second quotation is from Robert Spector, "How Nordstrom Became the Leader in Customer Service," ibid., October 15, 1995, p. 7.

Page 37: An Age of Self-Reliance: A week after writing this chapter, I received my copy of the *Harvard Business Review* (July–August, 1996), which reprinted as an "HBR Classic" Harry Levinson's 1981 article "When Executives Burn Out." Levinson has added a postscript to the article entitled "A New Age of Self-Reliance" in which he writes: "In today's world, we need to worry less about the next rung up the ladder and more about the variety of possibilities available to us should the ladder disappear and we find ourselves thrown back on our own resources." Although Levinson's postscript is too short to provide a plan for doing that, he obviously recommends an approach similar to the one we are taking here.

Page 38: Nineteenth-century writing on child rearing: Daniel Miller and Guy Swanson, *The Changing American Parent* (New York: Columbia Univ. Press, 1958), p. 40.

Page 38: Marvin Meyers: *The Jacksonian Persuasion* (New York: Vintage Books, 1960), p. 137.

Page 38: Ralph Waldo Emerson: From "Self-Reliance," in E. W. Emerson, ed., *The Complete Works of Ralph Waldo Emerson* (Boston: Houghton Mifflin Co., 1903–1904), pp. 46–47.

Page 40: Barry Diller: "The Discomfort Zone," *Inc.,* November, 1995, p. 19.

Part II

Page 47: Janis Joplin: *The Quotable Woman,* (n.a.), (Philadelphia: Running Woman Press, 1991), p. 34.

Chapter Three

Page 49: Don Marquis: Quoted in Evan Esar, ed., *The Dictionary of Humorous Quotations* (New York: Dorset Press, 1989), p. 136.

Page 50: Willa Cather: Quoted in Roslie Maggio, ed., *The Beacon Book of Quotations by Women* (Boston: Beacon Press, 1992), p. 80.

Page 50: Eric Hoffer: Quoted in Laurence J. Peter, *Peter's Quotations: Ideas for Our Time* (New York: Bantam Books, 1980), p. 512.

Page 52: Alexander Woollcott: Quoted in Esar, op. cit., p. 226.

Page 52: Audre Lorde: Quoted in Maggio, op. cit., p. 81.

Chapter Four

Page 61: Raul Fernandez: Lewis J. Perelman, "Why 'Barnstormers' Will Inherit the Knowledge Era," *Knowledge Inc.: The Executive Report on Knowledge, Technology and Performance,* July, 1996, p. 4. Perelman, previously cited as author of *School's Out,* is one of the few commentators who has a comprehensive view of the impact of the knowledge age on our institutions and values.

Page 62: Raul Fernandez: Ibid.

Page 64: Corning and Motorola: Ibid, p. 7.

Page 65: Haldane and Bolles: My own thinking owes a great deal to these two men, and anyone can benefit greatly from reading any of Haldane's books (a recent one is *Career Satisfaction and Success,* rev. ed. [New York: Amacom, 1988]) or Bolles's *What Color Is Your Parachute?,* revised annually (Berkeley, Calif.: Ten Speed Press). The latter book, which has taken on an almost biblical stature—in sales, in reputation, and in size—is the single best book on job hunting. If you've followed me this far, you know that I think that job hunting is passé. It's the measure of Bolles's understanding of his topic that his advice is, nonetheless, almost always worth following.

Page 66: It took me forever: This paragraph and the next originally appeared in modified form in my book, *JobShift: How to Prosper in a Workplace Without Jobs* (Reading, Mass.: Addison-Wesley Publishing Co., 1994), pp. 84–85.

Page 66: Douglas Richardson, Robert Saypol, Virginia Combs: Quoted by Tony Lee, "Disgruntled Lawyers Make a Good Case for Changing Careers," *Wall Street Journal,* July 23, 1996, p. B1.

Chapter Five

Page 72: Martin Buber: *The Way of Man, According to the Teaching of Hasidism* (New York: The Citadel Press, 1967), p. 15.

Page 73: Jean Girardoux: From his play, *Siegfried,* quoted in Rhoda Thomas Tripp, ed., *The International Thesaurus of Quotations* (New York: Harper, 1970), p. 466.

Page 73: Emerson: *Journals* (1836), quoted in ibid., p. 75.

Page 73: Heraclitus: *Fragments,* quoted in ibid., p. 76.

Page 73: Lawyers are often too competitive: Tony Lee, "Disgruntled Lawyers Make a Good Case for Changing Careers," *Wall Street Journal,* July 23, 1996, p. B1.

Page 74: For a book that explores the importance of work that engages the heart, see David Whyte, *The Heart Aroused* (New York: Doubleday Currency, 1994).

Page 74: Bell Labs: "Signs of the Times," (n.a.), in *Training & Development,* February, 1996, pp. 7–9.

Page 75: See, for example, Frank J. Sulloway, *Born to Rebel: Birth Order, Family Dynamics and Creative Lives* (New York: Pantheon Books, 1996).

Page 75: Deborah Tannen, *You Just Don't Understand* (New York: Ballantine, 1994) and John Gray, *Men Are from Mars, Women Are from Venus* (New York: Harper, 1993).

Page 76: Harry Levinson: See "When Executives Burn Out," *Harvard Business Review,* July/August, 1996. The afterword quoted in this book is on pp. 162–163.

Chapter Six

Page 82: Amy Quirk: She describes the business she and Eric Weiss founded in "Leveraging Expertise into Increased Sales," *Your Company,* August/September, 1996, pp. 18–19.

Page 83: Bill Gates and Microsoft: Gates's statement is from Malcolm Wheatley, "A Window on Bill Gates," *Human Resources* (U.K.), January/February, 1996,

p. 28. The other questions are taken from Ron Lieber's interview with Microsoft's director of recruiting, David Pritchard: "Wired for Hiring: Microsoft's Slick Recruiting Machine," *Fortune*, February 5, 1996, p. 123.

Page 83: Virginia Coombs: Tony Lee, "Disgruntled Lawyers Make a Good Case for Changing Careers," *Wall Street Journal*, July 23, 1996, p. B1.

Page 87: This point is made by Lewis Perelman in "Why 'Barnstormers' Will Inherit the Knowledge Era," *Knowledge Inc.* [Newsletter], July, 1996, p. 4.

Page 90: Alexis de Tocqueville: Quoted in *The Viking Book of Aphorisms*, selected by W. H. Auden and Louis Kronenberger (New York: Dorset Books, 1962), p. 56.

Part III

Page 99: Quoted in Louis S. Richman, "How to Get Ahead in America," *Fortune*, May 16, 1994, p. 49.

Chapter Seven

Page 101: Phil Wexler: Quoted in Griffith, *Speaker's Library of Business Stories, Anecdotes, and Humor* (Englewood Cliffs, N.J.: Prentice Hall, 1990), p. 207.

Page 102: Theodore Levitt: *The Marketing Imagination* (New York: Free Press, 1986).

Page 105: Atlanta airport: I owe this vignette to George Pendleton, who told me about the man, whom he had watched in action.

Page 105: Stanley Fukuda: Holman W. Jenkins, "Here's to Human Capital," *Wall Street Journal*, April 2, 1996, p. A15.

Chapter Eight

Page 120: Henry Ford: Quoted in Joe Griffith, *Speaker's Library of Business Stories, Anecdotes, and Humor* (Englewood Cliffs, N.J.: Prentice Hall, 1990), p. 377.

Page 125: Travel agencies redefining themselves: The quote and the three examples are from John Case and Jerry Useem, "Six Characters in Search of a Strategy," *Inc.*, March, 1996, pp. 52–55.

Page 127: Norm Brodsky: "Three Criteria for a Successful New Business," *Inc.*, April, 1996, p. 21.

Page 129: Black Oak Books: Gavin Power, "Bookstore's Tale of Triumph," *San Francisco Chronicle*, September 6, 1995, p. B1.

Page 129: Thomas Petzinger, Jr., "Gibson Does His Part to Make the Economy Safe from Cycles," *Wall Street Journal*, April 12, 1996, p. B1.

Page 130: William Gibson and Manugistics: From Petzinger's article cited above; and Amal Kumar Naj, "Manufacturing Gets a New Craze from Software: Speed," *Wall Street Journal*, August 13, 1996, p. B4.

Page 131: An outplacement executive: The subject of this story is Joan Blackman of Seagate Associates, Paramus, N.J.

Page 131: William James: Quoted in Laurence J. Peter, *Peter's Quotations: Ideas for Our Time* (New York: Bantam Books, 1980), p. 212.

Page 131: Japanese cars: Cited in Griffith, op. cit., p. 122.

Page 133: President of a New York–based clothing company: Quoted in Donna Fenn, "Homegrown Employees," *Inc.*, July, 1995, p. 95.

Chapter Nine

Page 136: Robert Schaen: Quoted in Janice Castro, "Disposable Workers," *Time*, March 29, 1993, p. 47.

Page 139: Andover Controls: Edward O. Welles, "Why Every Company Needs a Story," *Inc.*, May, 1996, pp. 69–75.

Page 140: Salon: Ibid., p. 75.

Page 154: Venture Initiatives: Stephanie N. Mehta, "Amateur Inventors Use Middlemen to Keep Day Jobs," *Wall Street Journal*, August 20, 1996, p. B2.

Page 155: For information on coaches, see Robert J. Grossman, "Game Plan," *Entrepreneur*, July, 1996, pp. 143–147; Jim Collins, "Looking Out for Number One," *Inc.*, June, 1996, p. 29; Carol Smith, "Putting a Coach in Your Corner," *Los Angeles Times* (special section called "Midcareer Checkup"), May 20, 1996, p. 7; and a newsletter published in Seal Beach, Calif., called *Professional Coaches and Mentors Journal*, the first issue of which (June/July, 1996) is the source of the information about Coach University. The sudden burst of information on this topic speaks volumes on the workplace changes that we are calling "dejobbing."

Page 155: See Lester A. Picker, "Hatch Ideas with Outside Advisers to Boost Profits," *Your Company*, June/July, 1996, pp. 32–35.

Chapter Ten

Page 160: Elinor Smith: Quoted in *The Quotable Woman*, (n. a.), (Philadelphia: Running Woman Press, 1991), p. 23.

Page 163: British Telecom: Company news release dated May 23, 1995.

Acknowledgments

This book began ten years ago—though I didn't know it at the time—with some work that I did at Intel and Apple Computer, where I noticed many people who didn't have what I then called "a real job." As I tried to figure out what that meant, I began to sound out people I met: had they noticed anything similar?

I pulled my impressions together into an essay called "Where Have All the Jobs Gone?" and sent it off to fifty people who thought about things like that. They gave me feedback. The essay made its way around. It was copied and passed along to others. And they gave me feedback.

Then I started giving speeches on the subject whenever I got the chance. More feedback. Then I pulled my thinking together into the book *JobShift*, and got more feedback still. Then *Fortune* chose to make an excerpt from the book the cover story for its fiftieth anniversary Labor Day issue. Lots more feedback.

Since that time I've presented the implications of the jobshift for individuals in a number of venues. There have been speeches and training programs at Hewlett-Packard, Motorola, AT&T, Shell Petroleum, Dow Chemical, Leo Burnett Advertising, and Amoco. I've tried out the ideas on audiences in France, Australia, Canada, and Brazil. Lots and lots more feedback.

Now I'm in the difficult position of having heard from and been influenced by so many people that I have lost track of the influence that others have had on my thinking and writing. A few stand out, of course.

My Addison-Wesley editor, John Bell, has been a wonderful combination of critic, supporter, and helper. My British editor, Nicholas Brealey, has been most helpful in saving me from the worst of my chauvinism. My agent, Jim Trupin, has been wonderfully encouraging and partisan on my behalf. My associates, Bonnie Carpenter and Maria Salvador, have kept the wheels going while I was busy writing, and my daughter and sometime associate, Sarah Bridges Parlet, has shared her experience and ideas. Beyond them I must take the coward's path of an alphabetical listing. Here goes:

Brian Baxter of Baxter's Books in Minneapolis, who fed me books even before I needed them.

Nancy Brown and Jim Meadows of AT&T, who gave me a full-scale chance to try these ideas out in a corporate setting.

Bill Daniels, a consultant in Mill Valley, California, who helped me to understand how the jobshift fit into the project-based world of Silicon Valley.

Chris Edgelow, Sundance Consulting, Edmonton, Alberta, who served as a sounding board as these ideas developed.

Debora Engel, 3Com, and Teresa Roche, formerly of the Grass Valley Group, who critiqued my ideas as they were developing.

Garth Johnston, Colorado Issues Network in Denver, who gave me several wonderful forums in which to try the ideas out.

Meryem LeSaget, a consultant and writer in Paris, who gathered an audience to hear and then edited the French edition of *JobShift*.

George Pendleton, of Washington, D.C., who helped me see the implications of You & Co. for those who have not fared well in the world of jobs.

Lewis J. Perelman of Alexandria, Virginia, who clarified the role of information technology in all of this.

Mark Powelson of San Francisco, who supported this project in its early stages and planned to create a PBS show on this subject.

Charles S. Savage of Boston, who helped me understand the historical and sociological context of these ideas.

Peter Van Sustern and his colleagues at Hewitt Associates, who are creating ways to make organizations based on these ideas work better.

To all of you, my gratitude.

And to Mondi, once again, my love and the dedication of this book to you.

Index

About the Author

William Bridges is the author of eight previous books. A former literature professor whose own career change first plunged him into the dejobbed world twenty years ago, he was originally trained at Harvard, Columbia, and Brown, where he received his Ph.D. in American Civilization in 1963. He founded William Bridges & Associates in 1981 to help organizations and individuals deal more successfully with transition.

William Bridges's training programs, speeches, and consulting have been used by several hundred organizations, including Pacific Bell, Baxter Healthcare, Intel, Apple Computer, Kaiser Permanente, Procter & Gamble, Hewlett-Packard, the U.S. Forest Service, Chevron Corporation, Kal Kan Foods, and McDonnell Douglas Astronautics. *The Wall Street Journal* listed him recently as one of the top ten independent executive development presenters in the United States. For more information on his publications and services, contact:

William Bridges & Associates
38 Miller Avenue, Suite 12
Mill Valley, CA 94941
Telephone: (415) 381-9663
Fax: (415) 381-8124
E-mail: wmbridges@wmbridges.com
Web: http://www.wmbridges.com

Made in United States
North Haven, CT
14 February 2023

32542465R00111